50
SUCCESSFUL
HARVARD
APPLICATION
ESSAYS

SIXTH EDITION

Also by the Staff of *The Harvard Crimson*

50 Successful Harvard Business School Application Essays
50 Successful Harvard Medical School Essays
50 Successful Harvard Application Essays, editions 1–5
55 Successful Harvard Law School Application Essays, editions 1–2
How They Got into Harvard

50 SUCCESSFUL HARVARD APPLICATION ESSAYS

SIXTH EDITION

*What Worked for Them Can Help You Get
into the College of Your Choice*

With Analysis by the Staff of *The Harvard Crimson*

ST. MARTIN'S GRIFFIN
NEW YORK

First published in the United States by St. Martin's Griffin,
an imprint of St. Martin's Publishing Group

www.stmartins.com

Library of Congress Cataloging-in-Publication Data

Title: 50 successful Harvard application essays : what worked for them
    can help you get into the college of your choice / With Analysis by
    the Staff of The Harvard Crimson.
Other titles: Fifty successful Harvard application essays | Harvard
    crimson.
Description: Sixth edition. | New York : St. Martin's Griffin, 2024.
Identifiers: LCCN 2023057900 | ISBN 9781250889720 (trade paper-
    back) | ISBN 9781250889737 (ebook)
Subjects: LCSH: College applications—Massachusetts—Boston. |
    Harvard University—Admission. | Exposition (Rhetoric)
Classification: LCC LB2351.52.U6 A13 2024 | DDC 378.1/616—
    dc23/eng/20231221
LC record available at https://lccn.loc.gov/2023057900

Our books may be purchased in bulk for promotional, educational, or
business use. Please contact your local bookseller or the Macmillan
Corporate and Premium Sales Department at 1-800-221-7945, exten-
sion 5442, or by email at MacmillanSpecialMarkets@macmillan.com.

First Edition: 2024

10 9 8 7 6 5 4 3 2 1

CONTENTS

Introduction: The Admissions Essay   ix
A Note from the Staff   xiii

I. IDENTITY AND SELF-REFLECTION

Neb F.   3
Una R.   7
Simar B.   11
Reza S.   16
Orlee M.   21
Oluwadunni O.   25
Marina S.   29
Marcus K.   34
Gil L.   38
Anant R.   42
Alexander D.   46

II. TURNING ADVERSITY INTO OPPORTUNITY

Shira H.   53
Raymond W.   57
Isabelle G.   61
Libby W.   65
Kyra F.   69
Simon L.   73
Michael T.   77

Contents

Lisber G.M.   81
Haley S.   85
Gred B.   90
Francisco M.   94
Ashley F.   98

III. INTELLECTUAL DESIRES

Kiran A.   105
Harry G.   109
Abby Y.   115
Stephanie B.   119
Nour K.   123
Manas K.   127
Jailene R.   131
Helen K.   135
Jinna C.   139
Michelle B.   143
Amy Z.   147

IV. INFLUENTIAL FIGURES

Jessica W.   153
Lauren P.   157
Ava B.   162
Kelisha W.   166
Connor L.   170
Bradley M.   174
Laura W.   178

V. PASSIONS

Sarika C.   185

Contents

Daniella Z.   189

Samantha C.   193

Georgina Y.   197

Rosanna K.   202

Clara N.   206

Billy B.   210

Gracia P.   214

Maia P.   218

CONCLUSION

Acknowledgments   235

INTRODUCTION:
THE ADMISSIONS ESSAY

A major change to the college application process since our last edition of *50 Successful Harvard Application Essays* is the more wide-spread acceptance of applications without standardized test scores following the coronavirus pandemic (COVID-19). As testing policies changed in response and many universities transitioned to adopting a test-optional model, the remaining components of the application are more heavily weighted and the personal statement has never been a more important factor in the admissions process. Test-optional policies have also led to many selective universities seeing an increase in applicants, so a particularly strong essay can help you stand out in this larger applicant pool.

The Common Application allows you to choose from a set of seven prompts and write a response within 650 words—a very limited amount of space to showcase yourself to the Admissions Committee. Therefore, learning how to maximize the space in your essay in relation to the entire application can allow you to put your best foot forward with the strongest possible essay. You want to avoid repeating the same information throughout the different sections of the application. The essay should highlight an aspect of your life that is significant to you but does not get to shine sufficiently in your grades, transcripts, recommendation letters, and resume.

When you are approaching the list of prompts offered by the Common Application, it may be daunting or seem impossible to know how to begin answering such open-ended questions. While there is no road map to writing the perfect essay, here are a few pointers and key structural techniques that can be applied to most successful essays.

BRAINSTORMING QUESTIONS

- What are some important things your reader should know about you?
  - Make a list of your best characteristics.
  - Ask yourself, How did you come to have these characteristics?
  - Was there a particular moment in your life when you developed or strongly demonstrated these characteristics?
- Whom do you interact with on a daily basis and what are your relationships with these people?
  - Ask yourself, What does their impact on you look like? Do you have a specific anecdote?
  - What positive sides of yourself does each person bring out?
- Are your emotions and reactions to certain situations relatable and demonstrative of maturity?
  - Who and what do you care the most about and why?
  - What makes you scared/nervous? How do you overcome that?
  - What makes you happy and why?
  - How have you overcome challenges, and how has that made you stronger?
- What is something you learned recently that piqued your interest?
  - Was it something interesting about yourself?

- Why do you think it piqued your interest? What can that say about you?

There are many different forms of personal narrative writing that allow an applicant's authentic voice to be heard by admissions officers. Typically, the best essays include an anecdote—a personal story or experience that proves a larger point about the applicant's character.

A great way to strengthen a personal narrative is to include a **Story Anchor**: a theme that shows up throughout the story. Story Anchors come in many different forms—objects, ideas, habits, people, words, memories, etc. Regardless, the best ones often center around personal relationships.

In this book you will find fifty essays that helped applicants secure an acceptance to Harvard College, one of the most selective undergraduate programs in the United States. Each student presents a different set of life experiences and character traits that led them on their path to success.

- In addition to the essays, we provided a profile of the writer including their hometown, high school type, GPA, standardized testing scores, and extracurricular activities. Each essay is also coupled with a brief analysis written by an editor of *The Crimson*, who will replay why a specific essay worked and what qualities and techniques made it compelling to the reader and admissions officers. The book concludes with some final tips and advice from the contributing writers.

A NOTE FROM THE STAFF

When writing the essay, the applicant may choose to disclose private parts of their life to the Admissions Committee. To respect all persons' and companies' privacy while maintaining the integrity of each essay, applicants had the option to choose aliases, disclose varying levels of background information, and redact identifying information with brackets ("[" and "]"). Thank you for your understanding.

I.
IDENTITY AND
SELF-REFLECTION

Neb F.

Hometown: Birmingham, Alabama, USA
High School: Public school, 350 students in graduating class
GPA: 4.0 out of 4.0 (4.6 Weighted)
ACT: 35
Extracurriculars and Awards: Bailey Thomson Award for Editorial Writing, National Merit Scholar
Major: Economics

ESSAY

"We need you to throw bombs."

It was a rather unorthodox way of telling me to write something controversial. With the deadline of our first issue rapidly approaching, the Co-Editors-in-Chief of my high school newspaper wanted to do something special, to set a precedent. Readership was the priority, and our best shot of increasing it was through the publication of a wide variety of eye-catching topics: the pervasive alcohol problem, the sexist dress code, and, of course, what would later be my opinion piece on our suburb's diversity, or rather lack thereof.

But I'm sure the newspaper teacher was beginning to have her initial doubts about my ability to run the section. While others already had an idea of what they wanted to write about, I—the supposed outspoken Opinions Editor—was the only one who didn't have a clue what to write about. Was I even deserving of the position if I couldn't speak my mind on simple school issues?

As the only junior awarded a section editor position, I somehow beat out seniors who had applied for Opinions Editor as their top choice. However, it was only a few weeks in before I fell upon the same self-doubts about writing for the paper that I had had as a sophomore the year before. Taking on the role of clueless newspaper newbie early on that sophomore year, I found guidance only in the sponsor's singular, resonating message: "Write about whatever interests you." It was supposedly as simple as that. No parameters. No governing rubric. No monotonous prompts. No, unlike the five-paragraph, formal essays and research papers we were programmed to churn out, my school paper presented an unprecedented opportunity of free will at hand, a creative free will that no other class had ever really emphasized firstmost. But not even I could capitalize on that kind of independence. That first year on the staff would mostly bear witness to the same "who, what, where, when, and why" features, news, and sports pieces, issue after issue, that demonstrated a skill in article writing, sure, but didn't quite showcase a writer's voice that was true to me.

That was to change, I resolved. This time around, I would write about the topic that was inherently bomb-laden: my heritage and my place in the predominantly white community where I had grown up in. Being, for a period of time, the only student of color in my elementary school, as well as the unfortunate recipient of countless, blatantly racist Asian impressions and jokes, would eventually shape a perspective that I was hesitant to speak openly about. Not anymore. There was too much at stake, an identity even. I could recognize that much. A long night of meticulous drafting would pass before giving way to a rough, but impassioned, opinion piece that spoke to the lack of both racial and political diversity that distinguished our community. The administration went on to censor out the more colorful aspects of all of our opinion pieces, but, for once, I could unabashedly take pride in the voice expressed in that draft. It was never about the stun factor, but rather about finding the courage to give my writing a stun factor in the first place.

Reflecting now on my involvement both on the paper as well as for other print publications, I've come to accept a certain credence. The opportunities writing offers are wide and plentiful in terms of self-expression at large, but the pursuit of topics that push you outside of your comfort zone makes the difference needed to write with a compelling conviction. As it turned out, this stated call to conviction came as the curious result of a simple request, a summoning of some internal, unrelenting voice capable of "throwing bombs."

REVIEW
What did the essay do well?

Neb does a great job of connecting two themes in his essay: growing as a writer and taking a proud stance on his identity. In this essay, we learn about how he overcame his hesitancy to express himself fully in the newspaper, which demonstrates his perseverance as well as his character. And while Neb makes his Asian identity central to the piece and mentions heavy topics, namely racism, he does not let that overpower the essay, keeping the message focused on his personal strengths and capabilities.

What could be improved about the essay?

The fourth paragraph, in which Neb walks us through his sophomore experience on the newspaper in order to contextualize his subsequent growth, is slightly unwieldy. The reader is led to navigate backwards in chronology and go through a different and retired mind-set. While the paragraph itself is well written, it could have been condensed to get to the main point: before his junior year, Neb didn't feel like he could capitalize on the unprecedented creative freedom the paper offered.

What made this essay memorable?

The hook of this essay—"We need you to throw bombs"—works really well. It grabs your attention right away without being obnoxious and the fact that it bookends the piece is a bonus. The hook shows off Neb's creativity and style, which nicely mirrors the actual content of his essay. Furthermore, the overall message of perseverance comes through the essay without being overpowering or cliché, which often happens with this theme of struggle followed by having to overcome said struggle. In essays such as this, something needs to stand out when reviewers have read this theme countless times over again, and the hook—as well as other unique stylistic choices—can be a strong way to accomplish this.

—Cara Chang

Una R.

Hometown: Brooklyn, New York, USA
High School: Private school, 96 students in graduating class
GPA: undisclosed
ACT: 35
Extracurriculars and Awards: Chamber music (piano), Science Olympiad, humor magazine, crossword club, Columbia University Science Honors Program, research at Memorial Sloan Kettering
Major: History of Science

ESSAY

The first word I ever spoke was my name. I was intrigued that my entire identity could be attached to and compressed into such a simple sound. I would tell everyone I met that my name meant "one," that it made me special because it sounded like "unique." When I learned to write, I covered sheets of paper with the letters U, N, and A. Eventually, I realized that paper was not enough—I needed to cover the world with my name, my graffiti tag.

This came to a screeching halt in kindergarten. One day in music class, I scratched UNA into the piano's wood. Everyone was surprised that I tagged my name and not someone else's. I didn't want someone else to suffer for my misdeeds. I wanted to take something, to make it mine.

Kindergarten was also the year my parents signed me up for piano lessons, and every aspect of them was torture. I had to learn to read an entirely new language, stretch my fingers to fit challenging intervals, use my arms with enough force to sound chords but not topple over, grope around blindly while keeping my eyes on the music, and the brain-splitting feat of doing this with each hand separately. Hardest was the very act of sitting down to practice. The physical challenges were more or less surmountable, but tackling them felt lonely and pointless.

I only fell in love with music when I found myself in a sweaty church on the Upper West Side—my first chamber music concert, the final event of a two-week camp the summer before sixth grade. I was nervous. My group, playing a Shostakovich prelude, was the youngest, so we went first. My legs shook uncontrollably before, during, and after I played. I nearly became sick afterward from shame and relief. I was so disappointed that I thought I could never face my new music friends again. From the front row, I plotted my escape route for when the concert finished. But I didn't run. I watched the whole concert. I watched the big kids breathe in unison, occupying the same disconnected body. I fell in love with music through the way they belonged to each other, the way they saw each other without even looking.

I stuck with that chamber camp. In the twenty chamber groups that have made up my last six years, I've performed in six-inch heels and nearly fallen off-stage during my bow. I've performed in sneakers and a sweatshirt, on pianos with half the keys broken and the other half wildly out of tune, in subway stations, nursing homes, international orchestras, Carnegie Hall, and on Zoom.

Chamber music doesn't work when everyone aims to be a star; it works when everyone lets everyone else shine through. It's more fun that way. A musical notation I rarely saw before playing chamber music is "una corda," which says to put the soft pedal down and play on only "one string," usually to highlight another player's solo. I don't need to be the loudest to breathe in unison with my friends, to create something beautiful. In that moment, I'm not just Una, I'm the pianist in the Dohnányi sextet.

I started to love music only when I realized it doesn't belong to me. I had to stop trying to make piano my own and take pleasure in sharing it. I learned that the rests in my part were as meaningful as the notes; that although my name means "one," I'd rather not be the "only." My favorite compliment I've received was that I made an audience member feel like they were sitting onstage next to me. This, to me, is the essence of chamber music. To pull your audience onto the stage, trusting your group isn't enough—you have to fuse together, to forget you exist. For a few minutes, you have to surrender your name.

REVIEW
What did the essay do well?

In her essay, Una is able to showcase an experience of growth, her passion for piano chamber performance, and her value of collaboration and working with others. The essay is well woven together to bridge her two primary topics: her name and unique identity, and her extracurricular piano. The technical writing and organization of the essay is also very strong, with a clear voice, easy to follow structure, and plenty of engaging details.

What could be improved about the essay?

The essay started off with red flags like stories that reflected less desirable personality traits and a focus on experiences all the way back to kindergarten. However, these early-warning signs are well resolved by the end to give both a good impression of the writer and a real sense of change. This is not a weakness on the part of this essay and is actually something done well since the author can be truly vulnerable by acknowledging their flaws, but addressing how they have changed and grown since then. However, readers should keep in mind that speaking about such dated experiences must tie back to the applicant in the current day, which Una does well in her description of where she has gotten in terms of chamber music, even performing on Zoom.

What made this essay memorable?

The entrance into the topic with the story of her name helps this essay stand out from other essays about piano or music in general. Without using it as an entrance, weaving it well into the body of the essay, and connecting it to her overall message, this essay would miss that unique quality and otherwise blend in with other similar essays.

—Isabella Tran

Simar B.

Hometown: Fremont, California, USA
High School: Private school, 200 students in graduating class
GPA: 4.0 out of 4.0 (4.72 Weighted)
ACT: 35
Extracurriculars and Awards: Medical Club president, Students Partner with Veterans Club president, Psychology Club president, Honor Council chair, varsity tennis, theater, John Near Scholarship, Presidential Volunteer
Major: History of Science

ESSAY

June 2nd, 2019. The birth of the new me, or "Simar 2.0" as mom called me. However, I still felt like "Simar 1.0," perceiving nothing more than the odd new sensation of a liberating breeze fluttering through my hair.

At age seventeen, I got a haircut for the first time in my life.

As a Sikh, I inherited a tradition of unshorn, cloth-bound hair, and, for most of my life, I followed my community in wholeheartedly embracing our religion. Over time, however, I felt my hair weighing me down, both materially and metaphorically.

Sikhism teaches that God is one. I asked mom why then was God cleaved into different religions? If all paths were equal, I asked dad, then why not follow some other religion instead? My unease consistently dismissed by our Sikh community, I decided to follow the religion of God: no religion. My hair, though, remained; if I knew my heart, then cutting my hair served no purpose.

Nevertheless, that unshorn hair represented an unequivocal beacon for a now defunct identity. I visited my calculus teacher's office hours, only to be peppered by incessant questions about Sikhism. He pigeonholed me into being a spokesperson for something I no longer associated with. Flustered, I excused myself to the bathroom, examining this other me in the mirror.

Why this hair? This question kept coming back.

I ransacked my conscience, and it became painfully obvious. Fear. Fear of what my conservative grandparents might think. Fear of what my Sikh family friends might say. Fear of what my peers might ask. This hair had usurped my sense of self.

So off it came.

A few days after crossing my personal Rubicon, I flew to India to meet my grandparents.

Breezing through the airport, I perceived something remarkably different about my experience: the absence of the penetrating surveillance that had consistently accompanied me for seventeen years. It was uncanny; I felt as an anodyne presence.

Apprehensively entering my grandparents' New Delhi home some eighteen hours later, I found myself enveloped in hugs. Savoring the moment, I failed to probe why. I recognize now that, in spite of their intransigent religious views, they appreciated that I had made a decision about my identity based on belief, based on being true to my evolving sense of self. I think my grandparents found that admirable.

A few weeks later, dad confessed, "I regret that you did not cut your hair earlier."

I have no regrets.

My hair made me work harder than everyone else simply because I looked different. Sanctimonious people lecture us on having pride in our differences, rarely considering the difficulties which being different entails. For example, a fake Facebook page created by an unknown schoolmate with my birthday listed as September 11th, 2001. Dealing with attacks fueled by ignorance never becomes easier, but such aggressions bolster my courage to face what other people think. In standing up for myself, I become myself.

On some level, I know appearances should not matter. Yet, in many uncomfortable ways, they still do, and they give birth to many disparities. Through the simple act of cutting my hair, I left the confines of intolerance, but my experience opened my eyes to those whose struggles cannot be resolved so easily. This motivates me to never be a bystander, to always energetically take the side of the persecuted in the fight against the powerful.

Over my years of shadowing, I have seen a healthcare system where patients receive inferior care solely on the basis of perceived race. Exposure to this institutionalized injustice motivates me to volunteer with a free health clinic to provide glucose screenings to the underprivileged. We must lead with personal initiative first, starting on the individual level and building from there. Only then can we bring about systemic change to reform the institutions and practices that perpetuate prejudice within medicine and without.

REVIEW

What did the essay do well?

Simar's essay focuses on one aspect of his physical appearance to explore different aspects of his Sikh identity. He starts his essay off with a glimpse into his initial thoughts about getting a haircut, shedding his unshorn hair and physical indication of being Sikh. Throughout the essay, he explores personal experiences and societal issues through anecdotal and introspective dialogue. He concludes his essay by returning to the conversation of what his hair symbolizes: difference. Simar touches on how differences in how people present themselves have led to ignorant discrimination and disparities on a systemic level, with his specific interest in the health care system.

Overall, the essay did a good job of using a metaphor to demonstrate Simar's personal conflicts in an intimate way, by also covering a range of different topics. The ending also effectively used the metaphor as a means to reflect and transition into framing how Simar would approach his academic and career goals moving forward.

What could be improved about the essay?

The essay attempts to weave together several different anecdotal experiences and dialogue, some of which could be much more effective if more focus was placed upon them. It ends in a somewhat abrupt shift into speaking to health care inequalities due to discrimination. Therefore, the essay is a bit rushed. The essay can be improved by perhaps focusing more closely on one or two anecdotal experiences that also weave in Simar's passion for health inequality to improve the flow and delivery of the story.

What made this essay memorable?

The hair metaphor as a means to demonstrate personal experiences as well as salient parts of society was clever. It is told in a sophisticated and astute way. Metaphors that are able to connect several important personal experiences and societal issues to a relatively normal topic (like hair) are quite memorable if done well.

—Linda Lin

Reza S.

Hometown: Los Angeles, California, USA
High School: Private school, 118 students in graduating class
GPA: 3.96 out of 4.0 (4.69 Weighted)
ACT: 36
SAT: 1510
Extracurriculars and Awards: Student government class president, class representative, head prefect. Student Mosque volunteer. Student and board member: BCIL Brentwood Center for Innovative Leadership. Eagle-to-Eagle program. Athletics: Water polo, soccer. Music: 1st Chair cello, section leader status, and student conductor. Vocal performing arts. Organization: Floating Doctors, AKDN Residential Summer Camps partici-pant, Brentwood School Admission Ambassador. Internship: Assistant to the Head Chef, Peppone Restaurant. Departmen-tal academic honors: Chemistry, Mandarin, orchestra. Dean's list. Benefacta Society Gold Distinction. Cum Laude National Academic Award. Book Award. Director's Award. National Merit Scholarship Program: Letter of Commendation. George Washington University Book Award. Presidential Volunteer Service Award: gold and bronze.
Major: Engineering Sciences

ESSAY

"You're Muslim?" It seems like a question which demands a yes or no answer, but I rarely answer in one word. On the lucky occasions I can, I respond with a whole essay.

In daily interactions, I never know the extent to which I should answer. It's a loaded question. I jump to the follow-ups: "What does this person want to hear?"; "How do I explain I am a particular Muslim, of many kinds?"; and then, "Is this person actually asking, or has he or she already decided who I am?" I feel the need to protect my identity.

Among other things, I'm a Shia Ismaili Muslim. The Ismaili sect is progressive: we are encouraged to participate in Ramadan, a typically required pillar of Islam, and pray three times a day, while most Muslims pray five times. My family decides when to attend mosque each week, while others go daily. Our Imam preaches personal choice and engagement with secular life. Yet, these complexities can be difficult to convey.

When I share with others that I'm Muslim, I feel an anticipatory sting because I know they'll see me as foreign. Even the word "Muslim" is stigmatized. Some say it only when they need to, others avoid the word entirely—though always, when it's said, the room goes quiet. I've learned I have to break the silence; I'm the only one who can.

As one of the only Muslims in my school, I'm often in a position where I must advocate for my faith, even when it makes me feel naked. In my immediate world, Islam is in an uncharted interstitial space where the status of Muslims has improved, yet prejudices persist. While unspoken, I still hear them. As I navigate the complicated space of being Muslim now, I must endeavor to discover and dismantle my peers' misconceptions—because they won't admit them out loud.

When curious minds ask about my religion, I have trouble finding the balance of what to say. When I say too little, I regret missing the chance to convey Islam's complexities, knowing my simple answer satisfies previous beliefs. When I say too much, I worry people will think I'm overprotective of my faith and won't be interested to learn more. And even when I say the right thing and my friends hear me, when they respond with shock or awe, I feel the most pain. They don't see my experience as normal, it makes me feel alien. Yet in reality, there are two billion of us and Islam's name derives from the Arabic word "salaam," meaning peace. Why must I explain myself so often? We come in peace.

And even then, though I often represent my faith, I am not the representative of it; no one person can be. I'd like to escape my given definition as just the "Muslim friend." I am a baker—when I was young, I learned my grandma's traditional Indian methods of making meat pies, and since then, spun-off her puff pastry recipe to make chocolate croissants. I am also an explorer—I collect key cards from every place I visit, from my homestay on the Vietnam rice paddies to a tent in the Serengeti in my family's homeland of Tanzania. My key cards remind me of my experiences abroad, and that traveling like a dry and ready sponge is the most effective way to soak up knowledge of foreign culture, in all three dimensions. I'm also a pretty "normal" high school kid. I enjoy going to parties with friends, though I don't drink, and I separately order a cheese slice, rather than peeling off pepperoni.

So I'm Muslim—it's not the only thing I am, but my faith gives me the confidence to be self-possessed and advocate for a three-dimensional view of all people. So when someone says, "You're Muslim?," I respond, "Yes, but you can call me Reza. Reza Munaf Abdulrasul Velji Shamji."

REVIEW

What did the essay do well?

Reza's essay begins with a clear hook that draws the reader in. "You're Muslim?" is, as he writes, a loaded question. In the next few paragraphs, Reza elaborates on his struggle to explain himself and his faith and meditates on to what extent that should be necessary. He makes several powerful statements in these paragraphs that touch on broader, more universal themes. Reza has clearly thought a lot about his identity and questions like whose responsibility it is to advocate for a group. The essay ends with Reza establishing that he is more than just his faith. While he is Muslim, he is also a baker, explorer, high schooler, and so much more. The second-to-last paragraph does a great job of humanizing the character of Reza and making him more relatable. While the topic of identity is a common one in college essays, Reza adds his own personal spin to it and demonstrates that he is someone who thinks deeply about the world around him.

What could be improved about the essay?

While already strong, Reza's essay could benefit from an additional layer of specificity. For example, if he recounted an instance of an encounter with a friend where he had to explain his religion or an example of something he would say, that might paint a clearer picture for the reader of what he is talking about.

What made this essay memorable?

The way in which Reza grapples with serious topics, such as identity and religion, conveys a sense of maturity and wisdom that shine through the words on the page. The ending was also quite powerful. In just a few sentences, Reza captures a lot of what he thinks makes him Reza and gives an impactful response to the loaded question he starts his essay with.

—Vivian Zhao

ORLEE M.

Hometown: Florence, Massachusetts, USA
High School: Private school, 201 students in graduating class
GPA: 93.2 out of 100
SAT: 1550
Extracurriculars and Awards: Editor-in-chief of high school newspaper, varsity swimming and water polo teams, Disciplinary Committee, Cum Laude Society, High Honor Roll, summa cum laude on National Latin Exam
Major: History & Literature and Human Developmental & Regenerative Biology

ESSAY

I'm hiding behind the swing door of the dressing room when I text my mom just one word: "Traumatizing!" I'm on a bra-shopping expedition with my grandmother, and just in case it's not abundantly clear, this trip was Not. My. Idea. Bra shopping has always been shrouded in mystery for me, and growing up in a household with two moms and two younger sisters hasn't helped one bit: One of my moms doesn't wear bras; the other proudly proclaims that her bras are older than me. A two-mom family without the faintest idea what a teenage girl needs—par for the course around here.

So when my 78-year-old grandmother volunteered to take me bra shopping, my moms jumped at the chance. Here I was with my frugal grandmother, outlet-shopping among the racks of intimates that aren't sized quite right, that have too much padding or too little . . . You can see my predicament, and it's no surprise that my younger self was confused by the words "wire-free," "concealing petals," "balconette."

The saleswoman called to my grandmother from across the store, "What cup size is she?"

"I don't know," my grandmother screamed back. "Can you measure her?"

Measure me? They have got to be kidding.

"I just don't want her to feel different," I heard my grandmother say later that day. "Kids this age can be so mean."

I love my grandmother, but she believes the world is harsh and unforgiving, and she thinks that the only path to happiness is fitting in. My grandmother had taken me bra shopping in a last-ditch attempt to make me "normal" because I was entering 9th grade at Deerfield in a few weeks, and she worried that I would stick out worse than the underwire of a bargain basement bra.

It's true—I'm not your typical Deerfield student. I'm a day student with lesbian moms who have several fewer zeros on their bank account balance than typical Deerfield parents. I'm the kid with a congenital foot deformity, which means I literally can't run, who will never be able to sprint across campus from classroom to classroom. I'm the kid with life-threatening food allergies to milk and tree nuts who can't indulge in the pizza at swim team celebrations or the festive cake and ice cream during advisory meetings.

But fitting in was my grandmother's worry, not mine. What my grandmother didn't consider is that there's no single way to fit in. I might be two minutes later to class than the sprinters, but I always arrive. I might have to explain to my friends what "having two moms" means, but I'll never stop being thankful that Deerfield students are eager to lean in and understand. I may not be able to eat the food, but you can count on me to show up and celebrate.

While I can't run, I can swim and play water polo, and I can walk the campus giving Admissions tours. My family might not look like everyone else's, but I can embrace those differences and write articles for the school newspaper or give a talk at "School Meeting," sharing my family and my journey. Some of my closest friendships at Deerfield have grown from a willingness on both sides to embrace difference.

On one of the first days of 9th grade, I sat down to write a "Deerfield Bucket List"—a list of experiences that I wanted to have during my four years in high school, including taking a Deerfield international trip and making the varsity swim team. That list included thirteen items, and I'm eleven-thirteenths of the way there, not because I have the right bra, but because I've embraced the very thing that my grandmother was afraid of. Bra shopping is still shrouded in mystery for me, but I know that I am where I should be, I'm doing work that matters to me, and fitting in rarely crosses my mind.

REVIEW

What did the essay do well?

This essay beautifully ties together a comical, unique topic with precise and punchy writing technique. The strong narrative voice consistent throughout brings out the author's personality, which aids the humorous description of her family and how unprepared her two-mom household is for the bra shopping. The essay is also stylistically reminiscent of a novel, with great use of dialogue to tell the story and a witty inner voice narrating other portions. Like writers whose goal is to engage their readers, the writing in this essay is similarly gripping and enjoyable to read. Orlee demonstrates that she is a great writer, humorous, and family oriented, but she is also vulnerable, yet strong when describing some of the challenges she has faced. Still, she orients all her challenges in a positive way that reflects well upon readers' perceptions of her.

What could be improved about the essay?

While this essay is very well written, one thing that Orlee does begin to do more in the second part of her essay is list more experiences rather than explore one experience in depth. Writers should be cautious not to fall into the trap of listing qualities over using experiences, allowing readers to come to their own conclusions about your characteristics from your actions. However, Orlee is able to avoid this folly, and instead of just listing qualities, she is instead listing multiple different experiences she has encountered. Personally, I think this makes the first half of her essay stronger, but the second half does not fall far behind.

What made this essay memorable?

Bra shopping is a particularly unique topic that sticks with the reader, as it is something very original and unlikely to pop up twice in an applicant pool. It is also a great choice because through that story and experience, the author provides bits of her personality, background, and family.

—Isabella Tran

Oluwadunni O.

Hometown: Clarksville, Maryland, USA
High School: Public school, 216 students in graduating class
GPA: 4.0 out of 4.0 (5.33 Weighted)
SAT: 1500
Extracurriculars and Awards: SkillsUSA, Student Government Association, National Honor Society, National Technical Honor Society, speech and debate, African Student Association, HOSA-Future Health Professionals, The Virago Project
Major: Neuroscience

ESSAY

Of the memorable moments in my life when I have discovered one of my passions, almost all of them involve my bright yellow Crocs. Buying rubber shoes in such a conspicuous color was not a spontaneous decision; it took me two months to choose. I had been stalking crocs.com, clicking between the color options, and asking for the unsatisfying opinions of friends before what felt like my rom-com "meet cute" moment: a girl wearing a black tracksuit walked past me in Crocs the brightest shade of yellow I had ever seen. That very week, I opened my laptop and decisively purchased a size 8 pair of "Lemon" Crocs. Ten business days (and two months to build up the courage to wear my eye-catching kicks out in public) later, my self-discovery began.

I was wearing my Crocs when I recognized the importance of activism in young communities. This revelation came on a Saturday in March 2018. I took a 25-minute train ride down to Washington D.C.

to participate in the March for Our Lives rally—my first protest. For all 25 anxiety-inducing minutes, my heart raced and my muscles tightened as I tried to ignore the probing stares from strangers wondering why I decided to pair yellow shoes with a green coat.

But my fears (both Croc and non-Croc related) quickly dissolved as I stood alongside activists that were my age; in front of a stage dominated by leaders that were my age; making me realize that the only thing stopping me from being a student activist, at my age, was effort. The young voices calling for change inspired me to step into my responsibility to use my voice to help those whose voices are being suppressed. I stood there for one hour, but what I saw was enough to encourage me to actualize my vision for a world where students are driven to engender social change through service. So, five months later, I co-founded The Virago Project (TVP), a student-led organization focused on building a community of activists like the ones I stood alongside in March. A "virago" is a woman displaying exemplary qualities, but the term has been twisted to demean assertive women. From its name to its activities, TVP is about redefining leadership.

After my day in D.C., I wore my Crocs to every student meeting TVP held. I wore them as we sold 150 handmade bracelets to raise funds for a local children's home and again when we posted colorful cards with encouraging messages all over my high school. Walking into rooms full of ambitious student leaders using TVP as a jumping-off point for their own service projects, I beamed as their gaze met my sunny shoes and then shot up to my equally cheery smile.

"Dunni, why do you wear such noticeable shoes when you lead these meetings?" asked one of our activists.

Pleasantly dumbfounded, I could only respond with a curious smile—it's not often that frivolous items lead to unintentionally philosophical inquiries. So, I held my tongue until the answer struck on a late-night in November 2019.

I wear such noticeable shoes when I stand in front of other student leaders because I want to model the kind of leadership that is as smile inducing, deliberate, and visible as my Crocs. TVP has trained me to be, above all, altruistic, and I love that I get to learn and model this with a generation of world changers. It took me two months to decide I wanted a pair of sun-colored shoes but only two seconds and a model to realize that I desired the option I'd once overlooked. Now, I realize that, to curious strangers, I am the girl walking past in Crocs the brightest shade of yellow they have ever seen. And I am delighted with the thought that I could be the one to break someone's cycle of indecision and social apathy.

REVIEW

What did the essay do well?

Oluwadunni first hooks the reader by explaining that all of the moments in her life where she discovered her passions were associated with her bright yellow Crocs. This causes the reader to become curious about what Oluwadunni's passions are and also how her unusual footwear might possibly be related.

Throughout the essay, Oluwadunni expertly intertwines the threads of her journey in activism with her bright yellow Crocs and how at each step her Crocs have helped her to discover something about activism or herself. Thus, Oluwadunni is able to communicate not only her accomplishments but also who she is as a person and leader in an interesting fashion.

Her closing sentences also provide a satisfying full-circle reference to her first paragraph: she is now the girl who might inspire other girls to get bright yellow Crocs and into activism and leadership. Not only does this provide a neat conclusion, it also helps the reader to understand what Oluwadunni's goals might be at Harvard.

What could be improved about the essay?

While overall it is a very effective essay, one thing that could be improved is how the question "Dunni, why do you wear such noticeable shoes when you lead these meetings?" is inserted into the essay. Currently, there is a sudden jump from a general description of TVP meetings to a specific interaction without situating it first, e.g., when was the question asked, at what kind of meeting?

What made this essay memorable?

Like the pair of yellow Crocs that the essay is about, the essay vibrantly conveys Oluwadunni's bright personality and her dedication to kindness and to being unapologetically herself while leading. This vivid imagery creates an association between Oluwadunni's writing style and lifestyle.

—Amy X. Zhou

Marina S.

Hometown: Miami, Florida, USA
High School: Public school, 760 students in graduating class
GPA: 4.0 out of 6.0 (5.447 Weighted)
SAT/ACT: undisclosed
Extracurriculars and Awards: Tutoring for Tomorrow, Odyssey of the Mind, Hispanic Scholar Youth Leadership Institute, Florida Power and Light Solar Research Center (Energy, Power and Sustainability Lab) intern, women's varsity swim team captain, The Conrad Spirit of Innovation Challenge, Mu Alpha Theta Math Honor Society president, Guatemala Medical Mission, Amigos for Kids, Science National Honor Society (VP), Hispanic National Scholar/USC host, National Economics Challenge Finalist (top 8) and State Champion (9th place), Odyssey of the Mind World Finals (State and Regional Champion), Ranatra Fusca Creativity Award, Brandeis Book Award (1st place), National Personal Finance Challenge (State level)
Major: Computer Science

ESSAY

It's 8 a.m. Dew blankets the grass under my bare feet as my small hands grasp the metal of the backyard fence. I lift my heels, summoning enormous power in my tiny lungs as I blare out a daily wake-up call: "GIRLS!" Waiting with anticipation for those familiar faces to emerge from their homes, my mind bursts with ideas eager for exploration.

Years later, at the corner of our yards, gates magically appeared; an open invitation connecting the backyards of four mismatched homes. The birth of the "Four Corners" inevitably developed into lifelong friendships and became the North Star in the lives of absolute strangers who have become family. As parents bonded at the gates, discussing everything from diapers to first dates, the kids took advantage of overlooked bedtimes and late night movies. Today, I launch into adulthood with the imagination, leadership, and confidence born from adolescent adventures.

Behind corner #1 lived the Irish neighbors, where I embarked on a culinary exploration of corned beef and cabbage served during the annual St. Patty's celebrations. My taste buds awakened with the novelty of a peculiar dish that seemed to dismiss the health hazards of sodium chloride, an element that conjures up mental images of chemistry experiments. With U2 playing on the speaker, and parents enjoying a pint of Guinness, adolescents discussed inventions that could lead us to a pot of gold; from apps that would revolutionize the music industry, to building a keg cooler from a rubber trash can (and yes, we actually tried that). Endless playtime and conversations fueled the gene of curiosity which molded my creative thinking and imagination.

Behind corner #2, vibrant Italians cheered on the creation of zip lines and obstacle courses, which taught me a thing or two about Newton's Laws of Motion. Body aches from brutal stops provided lessons in physics that prompted modifications. This inventive spirit during backyard projects required testing, redesigning, and rebuilding. I wanted to conquer the yard and use every square inch of it. My swimming pool hosted "Olympic Games," where the makeshift springboard I built would have made Michael Phelps proud. I dove into projects, disregarding smashed fingers and small fires. Through persistence and sheer will, repeated failures became a source of progress for all to enjoy. These lessons served me well when diving into the Odyssey of the Mind Competitions.

Corners #3 and #4, where Cuban roots run deep, entertained countless activities opening a world of learning and exploration. 1AM backyard stargazing encouraged my curiosity; the night sky like a blank slate, ready to be lit up with discovery. Through the eye of the telescope, I traced stars that were millions of miles away, yet filled my tent like fairy lights. Questions merged in a combinatorial explosion that only led to more questions. Could a black hole really cause spaghettification? Do the whispered echoes of dead stars give a clue to how old our universe truly is? Years later, at the FPL Energy, Power, and Sustainability Lab, conversations about smart grids, electric vehicles, and a possible colonization of the moon would take me back to that backyard camping, propelling my desire for exploration.

In my little pocket of the world, I embrace the unexpected coincidence that struck 20 years ago, when four families collided at the same exact moment in space and time. My Four Corners family, with their steadfast presence and guidance, cultivated love, maturity, risk-taking, and teamwork. Through my adventures, I became a dreamer, an inventor, an innovator, and a leader. Now, fostering my love for learning, spirit of giving back, and drive for success, I seek new adventures. Just as I walked through the magical gates of my beloved Four Corners, I will now walk through transformational thresholds to continue on a journey that began as a girl, at a fence, with a heart full of hope and a head full of possibilities.

REVIEW

What did the essay do well?

Marina's essay effortlessly uses imagery to flow ideas through her childhood and how they affect her now. With introductions like "Behind corner #1," we're imagining something out of a game show, allowing us to view each as a separate and equally important experience. The essay makes perfect use of the closing statement in each paragraph, providing an action statement that makes it plainly obvious what Marina gained through each experience (i.e., "propelling my desire for exploration").

The vibrant imagery and clear structure of the essay allow Marina to fill out the background of some of her personal qualities with tangible events and structures. This helps a reader connect with Marina on a deeper level.

What could be improved about the essay?

While this essay has great imagery, including the hook, it's a bit hard to connect the opening sentences to the rest of the essay. The flow of the essay is often more important than any stylistic choices thereafter. While it's not quite clear how waking up the neighbors ties into the meaning of the "Four Corners" fence, I think Marina could be better served using a comparison to the rather dull four corners intersection of Utah, Colorado, New Mexico, and Arizona. More effort should be put into the flow of the essay to ensure that it is well-rounded rather than only well written.

What made this essay memorable?

The most memorable part of this essay was the conclusion. Marina uses it to connect her story to her qualities one last time, allowing her to state a personal mission at the end. Finally, this is a very unique take on a simple concept—Marina turns simply befriending her neighbors into an opportunity for personal growth and development.

—Matthew Sheridan

Marcus K.

Hometown: Madison, Wisconsin, USA
High School: Public school, 2000 students in graduating class
GPA: 4.0 out of 4.0
ACT: 34
Extracurriculars and Awards: Mock Trial, SAGE (Sexuality and Gender Equality), National Honor Society, Wisconsin Youth Symphony Orchestra, State Chamber and Ensemble Solo Music 1st place, Foreign Language Department Award
Major: English and Women, Gender & Sexuality Studies

ESSAY

The Zoo

As late afternoon sunlight danced on my shoulders, I squished my eight-year-old face against the glass of the outdoor tank, eyes wide and searching for any signs of life. There! I scrambled from where I was seated, chasing the flickering sight of my prize. The otter darted away from me, his lithe body disappearing into a crack in the stones. I slumped against the wall, disappointed. Ever the HR representative, my mother saw my face and asked me what was wrong. I explained my frustration with the otters—they're so fun to watch, but they refuse to be seen. My mother leaned down, brushing a long lock of hair out of my face, and told me, "Sometimes, the animals get tired of being watched. They just want to be left alone."

I didn't think much of the otters after that. Until I became one.

In October of my sophomore year, I was four months into my

transition from female to male. I wasn't out to my extended family, my wardrobe was a haphazard mess of cargo shorts and skirts, and my voice was still, to my distress, annoyingly high. Being transgender at Middleton High School was no small feat—I stuck out in a sea of over 2,000 cisgender peers, and most of my teachers did not know how to deal with people "in my situation," as one put it.

One day, as I walked to my bus after school, I heard snickers from behind me. I turned around and saw a rowdy group of boys. One had his phone up, recording me. Everyone was laughing, and in an instant I knew they were laughing at me. I turned and walked away, doing my best to conceal myself from their view. The laughter continued.

I was the star of a humiliating show that I never asked to be a part of. I had become the otter. Their laughs kept ringing in my ears as I sat alone on the bus. I wanted to crawl inside myself and implode rather than think about going back to face them again the next day. My phone kept buzzing, but I refused to check it. It was only when I arrived home and checked those messages that I found that the video had been posted across social media for hundreds of my peers to see. It seemed like nothing, just a video of me walking, turning, and looking away. But their laughs were clear in the background, and I still understood the point of the video—look at the freak. Look at the new zoo exhibit.

Seeing that video, I realized that I couldn't allow myself to turn into what they saw me as. They wanted an otter, a punching bag that wouldn't fight back. I was not going to be their otter. The next day, I went to my first Sexuality and Gender Equality club meeting. I spoke to the administration about what had happened. I saved the video and showed people. I took control.

Those boys wanted me to believe that I was merely an exhibit to be laughed at, but now I know I live for greater things. I live for lattes, for courtroom closing arguments, for the pesto I make at work. I live for Black Lives Matter and #enough and Pride. I live for kayaking and summer camp, for the kids in SAGE and my younger sister. My classmates tried to dehumanize me, trample me, and mold me into their image of transgender people. Maybe they'll never see me as an equal, but that is their blindness, not mine. I do not live on display. I do not live in a zoo.

REVIEW
What did the essay do well?

In the first paragraph, Marcus starts with a compelling story that demonstrates his sense of curiosity, humor, and more importantly leaves the reader wondering how this anecdote might connect to the rest of the essay. In particular, Marcus uses a stand-alone sentence between the first and third paragraph to create this curiosity about how a person might possibly become an "otter."

In the third, fourth, and fifth paragraphs, Marcus answers this question as he connects the initial story to his experience transitioning in an unwelcoming environment. He captures his emotional journey using vivid descriptions and finally at the end of the essay loops back to his initial story by saying that he does not live on display and is not a zoo animal. These two ending sentences close out the essay in a powerful way and emphasize Marcus's bravery and determination for dignity.

What could be improved about the essay?

While the initial anecdote is effective, the essay could improve on dramatizing the story more such that it is more explicitly portrayed as negative to be an otter in the anecdote. In Marcus's essay, the otters move away from the glass to avoid being watched, but there is not much elaboration on whether such an action is bad or cowardly as is later implied. Thus, the effect of "becoming an otter" is not as strong.

What made this essay memorable?

Overall, Marcus very effectively captures the struggles that he went through during his transition and especially his courage throughout it. It is a very moving essay and demonstrates his character. However, he does so in a way that does not read as being character defining or all-encompassing. Rather than only expressing his struggles, he emphasizes the process in which he worked through them.

—Amy X. Zhou

GIL L.

Hometown: El Paso, Texas, USA
High School: Public school, 486 students in graduating class
GPA: 102.8 out of 100.0
SAT: 1310
Extracurriculars and Awards: TRIO UTEP Upward Bound, band, varsity ballroom dance, Multinational Business Academy, class president, National Honor Society, CLOSE-UP, Outstanding Principles of Business, Marketing, and Finance student, Best Student in Dual Credit Accounting, QuestBridge College Prep Scholar, Dell Scholar, Ysleta Independent School District Superintendent Scholar, College Board Opportunity Ambassador Program, United States Senate Certificate of Commendation, The State of Texas Certificate of Recognition, The IRS (Internal Revenue Service) Certificate of Community Service, Patrick Gilmore Award
Major: Economics

ESSAY

Growing up, I felt blindfolded—my path obscured by fear and uncertainty. The art of being blindfolded, however, is something I associate with being able to adapt. While blindfolded, you learn to use your other senses, not just your vision, to familiarize yourself with your surroundings. I have since relied on other senses to guide me further into the unknown of the future. These other sensory systems, my touch and hearing, guide me through the mystery of the college admissions process.

I was born into an immigrant household on the border of two different cultures. Lucky for me, I celebrate twice as many holidays, a Mexican version and an American one. Respectively, some of these are 16 de Septiembre and the Fourth of July, Día de Muertos and Halloween, and even celebrating Christmas and el Dia de Los Reyes.

I experienced my first cultural clash upon first entry into the United States. When I lived in Ciudad Juárez, Mexico, I watched SpongeBob on the local channel Canal 5. However, when I moved to El Paso, I would watch him on Nickelodeon, speaking what seemed like Chinese to me. Eventually, he became my best friend, a character who helped me learn English. Becoming bilingual had me saying things like "hoy no tengo homework," merging two languages into one sentence. Using my voice and my ears, this realization of the bicultural influence and melting pot within me encouraged me to open my mind, take off the blindfold, and see the possibilities that would await me.

As an incoming high school freshman, I became involved in extracurricular activities such as soccer and band. My performance exceeded everyone's expectations, so I was invited to multiple out-of-town tournaments and even state-level competitions. Because of this attention and success, my parents' absence in every event was noticed by my coaches, directors, and peers. Due to their immigration status and my fear of their deportation, I usually try to justify their absence by saying that they have to work. As I visit college campuses, alone and without my parents by my side, I am filled with a bittersweet feeling.

Although my parents are also blindfolded by my journey to create my path, they are still my cornerstone and number one fans. This is what has turned me into a resourceful person. With that being said, I have learned to reach out for guidance and insight from the Upward Bound program, my counselor, Ms. Villa, and my go-center specialist (College Admissions Advisor), Ms. Rodriguez. They have always lent me a helping hand, and their advice has been music to my ears. I still remember walking down my school gymnasium in kindergarten dressed in a cap and gown with a sash that said "Harvard." They made us pick a college from a list, but I did not even know what a college was, so I decided to "Eenie, meenie, miny, mo" it. Twelve years later, I can say that I am fluent in the language of college admissions. Now that I carved this pathway as the eldest first-generation student, my siblings and future generations of our family will be able to follow in my footsteps. Being the first in my family to enroll in and graduate from college has not only helped me become a mature person at a young age, but it will also break the family tradition.

For the longest time, I was afraid of being blindfolded. However, once my family decided to come to this country, it became a part of me. This has shaped my life and personality, but most importantly, my desire to succeed in the business world while reciprocating the aid I received from my community circle. As my senior year unravels, I can confidently say that what was covering my eyes has come off, and the journey I walked into with a disadvantage, I will walk out remarkably.

REVIEW

What did the essay do well?

Gil writes a really powerful essay, plain and simple. Their ability to create an analogy that seems to make little sense (being blindfolded) and turns it into a lens into which the reader can better understand not only Gil's experience but also the experience of many people who immigrate to the United States each year. In the third paragraph, Gil talks about the struggles of growing up with an unfamiliar language norm, as well as the experience of learning that language. What really separates this essay from the pack, however, is the conclusion, which ties in the blindfold analogy, Gil's experiences, and everything that was learned along the way, shaping who they are now.

What could be improved about the essay?

Although the blindfold analogy helps put Gil's experiences into a relatable perspective, the author does not continue to use it in the fourth paragraph. This paragraph has a strong topic (success despite struggles), yet it's a bit detached from the rest because every other paragraph seems to use the blindfold analogy. Furthermore, some explanations in the essay don't follow the overarching theme of the essay—for example, saying that their parents are their cornerstone and number one fans, which has made Gil resourceful. While this message is important, it detracts from the thematic elements of the remainder of the essay. Making sure that what's being said logically follows the explanation is crucial.

What made this essay memorable?

Gil's unique twist on their experience made the whole essay memorable. Throughout the essay, I and other readers were able to imagine someone wearing a blindfold and journeying through life, taking advantage of their other heightened senses. The imagery and relatable language help tie this essay to a real-life experience.

—Matthew Sheridan

Anant R.

Hometown: Marietta, Georgia, USA
High School: Public school, 600 students in graduating class
GPA: 4.0 out of 4.0 (4.82 Weighted)
SAT: 1600
Extracurriculars and Awards: Mock Trial, Cobb Youth Leadership, The Leukemia and Lymphoma Society, Smyrna Medical Associates, HOSA, Mu Alpha Theta, SNHS, NHS, WellStar Volunteer
Major: Human Developmental & Regenerative Biology

ESSAY

I thought I knew how to dress fashionably to school, but I hadn't yet met the Truth. I saw it for the first time last October during my daily meditation; it was an energy that pervaded all things, living and unliving; it contained the answers to life eternal, and I felt it. It was on that day that, lost in the transcendental spirituality of experiencing the entire expanse of the cosmos, I learned to truly wear the physical world around me. That Truth gave itself a corporeal form with eyes deep as galaxies and limbs light as a bucolic Mediterranean breeze, and with those, it unwrapped me from the cocoon I was unaware had existed in the first place. And with all the authority of destiny contained in its hands, it used that cocoon's silk to fashion me a new suit. So, armed with the verity of the universe as my tailor, I started to get dressed.

It was atop a hill in Florence that the Truth first extracted its needle from within the folds of its robes. As I looked out from atop that hill upon the serene, saffron-topped houses, upon the omnipresent greenery, I felt a curious warmth in the center of my chest, my heart beating fast as I saw true beauty. The Truth fashioned all that beauty of the scene, all the beauty of the world, into an emerald vest and buttoned it across my torso. In so doing, it imbued me with empathy, with a newfound ability to see that radiance in everyone around me. I was now able to understand people like never before, able to be a mentor, advisor, therapist, and a friend. Through these interactions, I met and befriended so many people, learning to hold each one close to my heart. And the Truth added all their new patterns, fibers, and decorations to my vest. So, bedecked with the love of family and dear friends, I put on my suit.

I got another suit-piece on a clear night in the Smoky Mountains when the Truth fit a thimble onto its fingertips and prepared again to sew. On a flat mountaintop, I lay down on a blanket, my eyes closed. When I opened them, my sister, lying next to me, grabbed my hand tight, for above us were the diamonds of the Milky Way, splayed across the sky. The Truth adjusted its spectacles, stole those twinkling gems, and slipped a celestial coat around my shoulders. Now, when I spoke, I learned to have the depth of space speak with me. When I walked, I learned to stand as tall and true as the stars above me. When I interacted with others, I learned to hide the introverted part of me that hid among the darkness, instead embracing the character of the talkative, glittering lights that shone through that darkness. Emboldened by the span of the universe around my shoulders, I walk into school.

I walk into school every day wearing an actual three-piece suit, my physical appearance reflecting the nature of my Tailor.

I've learned to stop along the way, to notice the people around me that I'm able to help. I can't solve their whole world's problems, but sometimes all it takes is to take that coat of confidence the Truth gave me and slip it onto their shoulders. As I walk through the halls of my school, I see my friends, feel the connection I have with them, and with each interaction we have, their pattern twinkles on my vest, right above my heart. Dressed in this suit, I have become a better person, but as I live on, my tailor surely has much more to give me. When the time comes, I'll return the coat to the skies and the vest to Mother Nature for another to discover. Perhaps, when the time comes, I can become someone else's tailor.

REVIEW

What did the essay do well?

Although the essay appears to be more on an abstract level, Anant does an amazing job of using vivid imagery and descriptions to successfully allow the reader to comprehend what he is attempting to say. The beautiful figurative language that is pervasive throughout the essay allows the tone of the story to be read seriously with a playful undertone.

The essay, in particular, highlights the creativity of Anant not seen elsewhere in the written or general application. The essay is an excellent place to describe or integrate elements that cannot be conveyed through the written application or letters of recommendation. Contrasting his extracurricular activities, his essay demonstrates Anant's ability to have interests other than that of academics. It gives the readers a lens into the other hobbies of Anant, in this case, fashion.

What could be improved about the essay?

The words "Truth" and "Tailor" are capitalized, which alludes to the fact that these topics are something of importance. Anant could have dedicated a sentence or two to fully explain the conception of "Truth" and "Tailor," which would have clarified the essay by a significant margin. Furthermore, there are some inconsistencies with "Tailor," which weakens the power of the capitalization. Anant could have improved his essay by explicitly stating a few epiphanies that would have sharpened his essay and made it less abstract.

What made this essay memorable?

Using fashion as a metaphor to fashion himself a new reality made this one of the more memorable essays. The astonishing imagery and details make this essay hard to forget. Just like the gorgeous suit that was described within the essay, the writing style of this piece is equally astounding. The essay also takes a considerable risk in being more abstract than the traditional essay, but this pays off in making the essay stand out to readers.

—Truong Nguyen

ALEXANDER D.

Hometown: Gainesville, Florida, USA
High School: Public school, 300 students in graduating class
GPA: 4.0 out of 4.0 (5.0 Weighted)
SAT: 1590
Extracurriculars and Awards: Varsity/travel team baseball, lab research, student body president, National Merit Semifinalist, Alachua County Sunshine State Scholar Conference Representative 2019, National Spanish Exam Gold Medal Highest Recipient (top 1%), student panel representative at Florida Mathematics Re-Design Institute
Major: Human Developmental & Regenerative Biology

ESSAY

The mouthwatering scent of beef broth brought back a flood of childhood memories as it wafted around me. After a 12-hour drive from Florida to Texas, the familiar smell meant I was in "bep cua bà," or "grandma's kitchen" in Vietnamese. Every summer when my family visited my grandparents' house, my grandma always had a steaming pot of pho ready for us when we arrived, and this time was no exception. For my family, pho was more than a Vietnamese delicacy: it symbolized bringing us together over a warm, hearty meal. This specific visit, however, came with a change of perspective; as a young adult who was now conscious of his cultural roots, I wanted to learn more about my heritage by learning how to cook pho from my grandma.

As she boiled the water, my grandma stressed to me, "Every

bowl of pho needs a strong foundation: the broth." Without a good broth, she explained, none of the other ingredients mattered. As I stood over the boiling pot, I thought about my own foundation: my family. My parents immigrated to America after the Vietnam War with nothing and had to work tirelessly to accomplish the celebrated "American Dream." From taking me to a 7 a.m. student government fundraiser or a 10 p.m. baseball game in a city five hours away, I would not have been able to participate in these activities, which I consider an integral part of my identity, without their support. Being fortunate enough to have a strong foundation in my life has allowed me to be a strong foundation for others. For example, as an upperclassman on my varsity baseball team, I strive to be available for my teammates. Last season, when a younger teammate was struggling in a few games, I stayed back after practice to work with him on his fielding before driving him home, even though he lived almost an hour away. This small gesture was a reflection of my attempt to build a strong foundation for others.

As I watched the broth simmer in a giant pot that my grandma had continuously stirred for two days, she imparted another bit of wisdom onto me: making a great bowl of pho was also all about balance. Simply taking a great broth and indiscriminately adding to it would not suffice; each of the ingredients had to be in perfect balance with each other. Balance was never really something I considered until recently, when I experienced the struggle that can come from its absence. When I suffered a stress fracture in my lower back a few years ago that left me unable to play baseball for the foreseeable future, I felt as if suddenly a major part of my identity had been stripped away. I struggled with this new reality for a while until I realized I could fill this temporary void by acting as a mentor for my younger teammates. Additionally, with my newfound spare time, I was able to further develop my interest in Mu Alpha Theta, which gave me a new, enriching opportunity to compete in mathematics competitions. By the time I was finally cleared to play, I had developed a fresh appreciation for the importance of maintaining a balance among all the activities I did, as I had experienced firsthand the empty feeling of having this balance stripped away.

While putting the finishing scallions in the bowl, I reflected on the delectable meal I helped create and realized that what had started out as me simply wanting to learn more about my heritage became something more poignant: an introspection. Although there may not be a single perfect recipe for pho, by applying my grandma's cooking principles in my everyday life, whether it be in baseball, my volunteer lab experience, or my service trip to Guatemala, I hope to be able to make a "bowl of pho" that is perfect for me.

REVIEW

What did the essay do well?

What this essay does particularly well is showcase the author's personality and perseverance throughout the personal statement. This high schooler takes this opportunity, one that lies outside of the initial written application, to highlight attractive skills that he has acquired throughout his life, such as perseverance and community building, just to name a few.

The essay's imagery of the grandmother and her grandson, leaning over the boiling pho broth, is one that also demonstrates the author's writing skills. In addition to showcasing who he is, the author also demonstrates how he can think abstractly, connecting two things that don't seem initially intertwined—such as his culture's food and his experiences in high school.

What could be improved about the essay?

There are some small choices that could polish this otherwise complete essay. Getting rid of the double quotation marks used and breaking the essay down into more paragraphs could make it flow better. For a reader and reviewer, very few, but very large, paragraphs can be a lot to digest in a short amount of time. For example, especially in the second and third paragraphs, thematic breaks could be implemented in order to make the essay more palatable. One place that this would work well is immediately before the line that begins with: "Balance was never really something . . ."

What made this essay memorable?

This essay puts a unique spin on a common essay theme about family. Because so many high school students write about their connection to their family and culture's values, it is difficult to write a personal statement that differentiates itself from the others. What makes this essay unique is its specificity. By grounding the essay in the grandmother's bowl of pho, the author can then use the food as a metaphor for his struggles and experiences thus far.

—Penelope Alegria

II.
TURNING ADVERSITY
INTO OPPORTUNITY

Shira H.

Hometown: Hanover, New Hampshire, USA
High School: Religious private school, 68 students in graduating class
GPA: 3.96 out of 4.0
ACT: 34
Extracurriculars and Awards: Varsity volleyball, Mock Trial; prayer group coordinator
Major: Social Studies and Religion

ESSAY

I could do a standing backflip before I could solve X + 2 = 3. From age two to 14, gymnastics consumed my world. I spent upwards of 14 hours in the gym every week, getting to know my coaches and teammates better than my teachers and classmates. In favor of gymnastics meets, I skipped school dances, religious services, and family events. I consistently placed first at these competitions, eventually winning five state titles and reaching the second-highest level of competition.

Gymnastics was a rigorous cycle of immense gratification. I would spend hours falling off the balance beam and clambering back on it, until I finally perfected a skill. Immediately, I would ask the coach for the next skill to learn, and I would begin the cycle of falling and perfecting again. I was so invested in this cycle that I ignored the intense back pain I was experiencing until it became unbearable.

When my doctor told me, right after my Bat Mitzvah, that I had a stress fracture in my back, both my gymnastics career and my identity suddenly seemed in jeopardy. Fully committed to my sport, I opted to take the most aggressive recovery path, wearing a plastic brace 23 hours a day for three months. But in my newfound spare time, I continued the Jewish studies I had begun before my Bat Mitzvah ceremony. Five months later, I was competing again at the same level.

Then I re-fractured my back, and my gymnastics career was over.

To say that I felt directionless would be an understatement, but my Jewish studies were a light in the confusing darkness which compelled me to dive more deeply into my Jewish identity. I sought out a tutor who helped me become fluent in Hebrew in just two years, began teaching at my Hebrew School, and started leading Shabbat services regularly. Judaism began to take the spot that gymnastics once had in defining my identity.

Unfortunately, living in rural New Hampshire, the rigor that I had come to cherish in the gym was lacking in both my Jewish community and my high school. In search of this rigor, I began independently researching schools that would nurture my passion for Judaism and scholarship. I fell in love with Gann Academy, a school in Massachusetts with a dual Jewish/secular curriculum. Gann both fulfilled these criteria and curated a community of independent Jewish seekers. Unfortunately, it was not a boarding school. Undeterred, I jumped at the opportunity to move in with family acquaintances in the Boston area, living with them during the week and commuting home twice a month.

Gann opened up a whole new world for me, a world of independence, exploration, and deep grappling with my identity. Not only did living away from home mean driving, cooking, and doing laundry independently, but it also allowed me newfound independence in my Jewish practice. I dove into extra advanced classes in both Jewish and secular subjects and began exploring different Jewish modalities, ultimately landing on a set of practices that, while more observant than my family's, I found to be more spiritually compelling. Still motivated by a challenge, I began seeking out leadership roles in the school, such as spearheading a project to promote cooperation and inclusivity between prayer groups, coordinating the religious aspects of our annual retreats, and leading services.

The end of my gymnastics career was crushing at the time, but looking back, I am grateful for the experience. Being an active participant in a vibrant Jewish community allows me to grow from and with others in an empowering and dynamic way that I hope will only be enriched in college. My injury enabled me to develop a new identity that revolves around Judaism, which neither broken bones nor age can take away from me.

REVIEW

What did the essay do well?

Shira's essay begins with a dynamic hook where she draws in the reader by contrasting an impressive skill set she once had to a seemingly simpler mathematical task. Her essay demonstrates a clear and easy to follow structure and does a great job of guiding the reader from a passion to which she was deeply committed, to the challenge and ultimate turning point where she had to adapt, and finally to a new interest that allowed her to grow and represents her as an applicant.

What could be improved about the essay?

While the essay does a great job of painting multiple aspects of Shira's personality and life by detailing her exploration of Jewish studies and her passion towards gymnastics, the description in the second half of her essay is a little bit basic. The first section of the essay demonstrates a beautiful storytelling voice that gracefully articulates her commitment to gymnastics. In comparison, focusing on Gann Academy and specifically how going to this school opened this door to a new interest for her in the second half of the essay feels less effective because the focus is shifted away from the writer herself at times.

What made this essay memorable?

Unlike many other personal statements that address a challenge one overcomes, Shira's essay uses this topic to structure her essay in a way that informs the reader of some values and lessons she collected while pursuing her passion in gymnastics, which she can bring to college as a student. Additionally, Shira's exploration of religion delves into a very different side of her personal life, which helps to portray her diverse interests. Because of this, readers are left with more than just the author's interests, but how they have all combined to shape her as both a person and a student.

—Isabella Tran

Raymond W.

Hometown: Watertown, Massachusetts, USA
High School: Public school, 150 students in graduating class
GPA: 3.9 out of 4.0 (4.497 Weighted)
SAT: 1480
Extracurriculars and Awards: Drama/theater, Gender and Sexuality Society, a cappella, National Honor Society inductee, Cum Laude Society inductee
Major: Chemistry

ESSAY

In July of this past summer, I got an unexpected call informing me that my mother was hospitalized after an overdose. I maintained my composure over the phone while receiving the news, but once I hung up my resolve began crumbling. Panicking, I patched the holes that formed in my facade, only allowing myself enough tears for others to think I was reacting appropriately.

That day, and nearly every day for a week, I went to the hospital over three hours away to see her. During the long, sweltering drive one of those mornings, there was a period when I passed by miles of black-eyed Susans lining the median and sides of the highway. Although they were sparse at first—specks of beauty in an otherwise unassuming landscape—they soon grew to number in the thousands, obscuring the dried brown grass underneath with their golden petals.

Until then, I was outwardly stoic; it was the first coping method I always used, even if it wasn't the best. However, this sight was one that I, a bona fide city slicker, had never witnessed before. It grounded me, which made me suddenly hyper-aware of my and others' mortality, reawakening the emotions that I suppressed. I sobbed for the rest of the ride, unable to think of anything but my mother's impending death.

My mom was the strongest person I've ever known, and the most willing to take control of her own fate—she passed down her resilience to me. It was in my blood to be strong. The last time I left her bedside, I tried so hard to wipe my tears and never look back. I wanted to be the best version of myself that I could be, in part to fulfill my destiny as my mother's child, and that person couldn't spend the rest of the summer crying. I needed to focus on life without her.

The problem with this was that I became excessively self-critical. I chastised myself for stress-induced weight gain, for taking time off from my job, for not having the energy to do chores—instead of feeling motivated by my criticisms, I felt hopeless by them. By not allowing myself the chance to heal, I tore the wound open wider.

In my downtime, I spent a lot of time ruminating. In August, by a stroke of luck, a thought that crossed my mind was, "What would she want me to do?"

In turn, this became, "Would she want me to do this to myself?"

And I knew the answer to that was a resounding no. My mom was a proponent of eating whole pints of Ben & Jerry's when you're sad. Even though I'll settle for half a pint now, remembering these things made me realize I could be less than perfect sometimes, especially now.

At some point, I developed the false notion that ambition and vulnerability were mutually exclusive—if you allow people to see you when you're weak, then you are weak and incapable. But that notion left me bitter and pessimistic. If anything, it destroyed my ambition—if I'd lose so much if I failed, then what was the point of trying?

To realize that I wouldn't be held back by my feelings took seeing it done—when I went back to work and school, I was welcomed with an endless outpouring of support from everyone I knew. Support for me emotionally, yes, but also for my dreams and aspirations as I move toward life after high school. I believe this will be my best year yet, despite the setback.

When I walk home each day, I pass by clumps of the little yellow flowers in the yards of my neighbors. It's bittersweet; I miss my mom so much it hurts sometimes, but the blooms remind me to strive toward the sky and open my heart to others like they open toward the sun.

REVIEW

What did the essay do well?

This essay wrestles with a particularly troubling topic: the death of an immediate family member. Grief and loss are not easy to write about, and these themes are especially difficult to articulate in the context of a college application. This author effectively takes a traumatizing experience and explains how he confronted it and grew because of it.

Raymond demonstrates how he adapted to his mother's situation and how he learned to keep on living. This is done especially well by concentrating on small symbols, such as the little yellow flowers, as a sign of hope.

What could be improved about the essay?

This is not an issue with this essay, but instead a note about readers who might be inspired by this one and consider writing about adversity. Adversity is a theme that many high school students gravitate towards writing when it comes to the personal essay. Some who haven't experienced adversity even feel that they do not have anything to write about. This is a common misconception. Personal adversity essays are prevalent in college applications because it is just another way to show colleges that you are capable of struggling through hard times and eventually overcoming them, but it is not the only topic option and if selected it should be written with care and intention.

This essay did a great job of delivering a powerful narrative, but it could be stronger with changes to the structure. The writer alternates between describing ongoing events and past emotions, which makes the essay feel disorganized at times and harder to follow for a reader.

What made this essay memorable?

It is the specificity of details like the little yellow flowers that makes this essay memorable. It allows the reader to access the writer's thought process and understand who he is as a person—which is the whole point of the personal statement in college applications.

—Penelope Alegria

Isabelle G.

Hometown: Queens, New York, USA
High School: Private school, 96 students in graduating class
GPA: 4.0 out of 4.0
ACT: 35
Extracurriculars and Awards: Student journalism, cultural dance, school productions
Major: Economics

ESSAY

Breakfast after church is a Sunday staple in my family. We're not allowed to eat beforehand, so right after Mass ends, my sister and I race to the bagel shop only to inevitably wait in a long line. Often when we reached the cashier, we'd find they were out of plain bagels. It was a perennially difficult decision: pick from an assortment of non-plain bagels, or wait another 20 minutes for new plain bagels.

People's bagel choices tell you everything about them, and I was a plain bagel girl through and through. Even when faced with 20 extra minutes of hunger, I decided to leave the sweet bagels for the adventurous, the savory for the straightforward, and the "everything" for the indecisive. I came for plain bagels, and I would get them, no matter the wait.

After a long wait, the warmth of the freshly-baked plain bagels radiating through the paper bag assured me my patience was worth it. Being a plain bagel girl means knowing exactly what you want—

no more, no less. It means that I'm in control of my decision-making and always end up satisfied.

In senior year, my teacher graciously brought bagels to our class. Upon approaching the bag, however, I found there were no plain bagels left. Instinctively, I retreated. But my teacher stopped me and advised that I break from my comfort zone. Reluctantly, I chose an egg bagel, preferring its odd yellow shade to the surrounding sweeter variety (who wants a french toast bagel anyway?). My first bite introduced me to a new world: this sweet and savory egg bagel flawlessly balanced the worlds of the adventurous and the straightforward.

My willingness to try an egg bagel didn't lead to a phase of food experimentation, but it did make me see that I could be more spontaneous than my plain bagel self might allow.

Before high school, you could never spot me on a dance floor; I much preferred to watch from the audience. But in my freshman year, I joined the dance department of my school's annual production of S!NG on a whim.

As soon as I tried the first move, I knew the decision was worth it. I enjoyed diligently practicing routines and adding my own flair, satisfying my tendency to prepare thoroughly while also fulfilling my desire to explore the realm of dance. Eventually, I excelled so much that the directors chose me as their successor—a position that has strengthened me as a dancer, leader, and person. Though I relished my newfound sense of spontaneity, my plain bagel girl roots helped me to effectively manage others' dancing. I tirelessly choreographed and re-choreographed each step and count of a routine, no matter how long the detailed revisions took. During practices, I analyzed the dancers' movements and refined them to what could only be described as plain bagel perfection.

Sometimes the moments when I thought I needed to be in control to be successful were when I needed to be more spontaneous. In my first year being director, I was unfamiliar with managing a multitude of variously skilled dancers. Shedding my fear of being an inexperienced leader was difficult, but I soon learned to open myself to others' advice about describing moves and maintaining the beat. Together, through sometimes spontaneous practice sessions and spurts of inspiration, we worked to adapt the choreography to accommodate all dancers.

I revel in the contradiction that is my simultaneous meticulousness and spontaneity: my egg bagel epiphany. I can count on myself to prepare thoroughly to optimize my potential, no matter how long it takes. But I can also trust myself to make the most of the unknown and stay true to myself while doing so. It's what makes me multidimensional; it makes me a young woman no longer defined by her bagel choices but rather by her versatility and what she can do with it.

REVIEW

What did the essay do well?

Isabelle begins her essay with a personal touch, giving us a lens into her Sundays. She then transitions from her Sunday mornings into a common dilemma of "choosing a flavor," which creates the tension in her story and generates stakes for the readers. She turns a rather mundane moment of picking a bagel and sticking to a safe flavor into a story of growth and self-realization.

Her epiphany with the egg bagel helps her directly tell the admissions officers that she has grown. She realizes her flaws and shows how she realized it through something as common as a bagel, highlighting her creativity and proving her ability to think outside the box.

What could be improved about the essay?

Isabelle focuses on stepping out of her comfort zone, which is a cliché topic. She ameliorates this by using bagels and dancing as metaphors for the story. However, she could have perhaps refined her metaphors and takeaways from the essay better by incorporating different moments of growth throughout the essay instead of telling it to the readers towards the end. As it stands, she highlights her growth through S!NG, but she could have demonstrated other moments of growth throughout her high school career.

What made this essay memorable?

Using the humble bagel as a metaphor for personal growth made this a very memorable essay. Isabelle carefully navigated this metaphor, not going down a common structure of how one event sparked creative experimentation for all subsequent events. Instead, Isabelle stuck with the plain bagel as her primary metaphor. Through her doing so, the reader is able to see how the attributes of the bagel still reflected who she was on the inside, and it helped to deliver a more original essay. Furthermore, by using a rather informal tone, Isabelle makes the readers comfortable, which helps her transition from bagels to dancing.

—Truong Nguyen

LIBBY W.

Hometown: Boston, Massachusetts, USA
High School: Private school, 96 students in graduating class
GPA: 4.42 out of 4.0
SAT: 1560
Extracurriculars and Awards: Captain varsity rowing team, school newspaper sports editor, Babson ACTIVATE Entrepreneurial Academy, Model UN, City of Boston Mayor's Youth Council, BLS Franklin Medalist (awarded to top 7 graduates), National AP Scholar, National Honor Society, National Latin Exam Medalist, National Spanish Exam Medalist
Major: Economics

ESSAY

The wind is unapologetic, as is the rain. A huddle of us paralyzed by disbelief, fists pounding on the soggy grass. An exasperated line of snot on my soaked racing layer. Our rival, Brookline, had just won States. Twenty-four hours ago, our boat had defied precedence and advanced to the grand finals of the NEIRA Championships to be 24 seconds faster than them, but today we were collateral damage of the elements. How did we lose?

In that moment on the ground, I wondered if we could ever recover. To my dismay, suddenly it hit me—my father had also hit rock bottom, albeit many years ago, but had never stood back up. The ghosts of his failure haunted me holographically, and they threatened to seep into my wounded morale.

He is everywhere in my life, and yet he is nowhere to be found.

Sixteen years ago, his dreams for entrepreneurship led him to China. However, this genius, top of his class, Tsinghua Math Major unconsciously defeated himself by ignoring the takeaways from his failures. His daytime reverie for acquiring wealth to impress us, like a dog returning the ball in a game of fetch, remains unrealized to this day.

My father never comes back because, in short, he can't face his underachievement of the great expectations for which he lives. He views "never giving up" through a romanticized lens, aching to be defined by one success, any success! I may not possess the shovel to dig him out and offer him a hand at this moment, but I must comprehend his downfall. Although his blind optimism is honorable to an extent, I realize the misleading appeal of dwelling on what could've been, since it eroded his sense of reality. Driving on the road to his dreams, this man assumes that his pursuit has no speed bumps, foreseeing no failures. However, I know better than to expect a straight shot.

From that day on, I determined to paint my setbacks as the impetus to my pursuit of the seemingly unattainable. Contrary to his example, I am letting myself ride every bump in the road, knowing that each one brings me closer to the realization of my goals. After all, if I couldn't move on from this blow, then how would I be any different than him? I crawled back up, and we wiped away our tears.

A year after the fated States, my teammates and I leave it all on the NEIRA race course, repurposing the pain of last year's failure into the sprint. The coxswain's voice fills our ears, echoing my remark: "I WANT TO FEEL THE FLORIDA SUN!" Goosebumps on our skin. Split seconds later, we cross the finish line to cinch that qualification spot to Nationals. 2 weeks later, we packed our bags for Florida. We're finally under the sun. And as one of the only public school teams in the 1st Varsity 8+ event, I could not be more thankful for that failure one year ago.

Even though it never clicked for my dad, I now appreciate the power of emotionality—embracing every feeling, good or bad, that accompanies failure. Such a confrontation won't provoke me to shrink at the pursuit of something "too lofty". Rather, it will propel me with an understanding of all that I am capable of. I will fall every so often, and that's okay. Like my mom told me in first grade, the wounds from falling onto the cement during recess will eventually become scars, then heal. They won't disappear (I actually still have a banged up knee), but I'm glad that they exist. What matters is that I stood back up. After all, what's the fun in staying on the ground? I have a lifetime of mileage to go.

REVIEW

What did the essay do well?

Libby's essay navigates a compelling personal story about her experience with failure through rowing and her father's struggles for success through a clear and well-organized structure. She starts by recounting an unexpected loss at a championship race, providing detailed imagery of the conditions and agony of defeat. Libby then reflects on the challenges her father faced and his inability to recover. The parallel between her own setback and his provides a smooth segue to demonstrate her personal growth. Libby realizes that her father's sole focus on success distances him from reality, making him unable to treat failure as a natural part of success. Learning from this, Libby returns to herself, detailing how she was able to overcome her disappointment and find success a year later. The essay concludes with a thoughtful discussion of taking failure and success as they both are: intertwined.

What could be improved about the essay?

The initial transition between the two themes could be smoother and more cohesive. The essay rather abruptly jumps from the rowing loss to her father's failures, which can be slightly confusing at first. Greater specificity in her father's struggles with failure can give a clearer sense of his downfall and how that translates to Libby's own takeaways. Libby's resilience arc is not explored so much in detail—exploring how she bounced back and differentiated herself from her father would give the essay a stronger finish.

What made this essay memorable?

Tying rowing with her father and conveying a powerful message about failure and success make this essay stand out. Libby took the theme of "learning from failure" and crafted it into a nuanced essay that highlights her strong perseverance and resilience. Moreover, Libby remains transparent about her fluctuating emotions, which delivers a much more raw and personable essay.

—Derek Chang

Kyra F.

Hometown: Saratoga Springs, New York, USA
High School: Public school, 531 students in graduating class
GPA: 97.82 out of 100
SAT: 1520
Extracurriculars and Awards: French Language Award x3, English Department Award x3, Latin Language Award x2, Technology Department Award, Math Club, French Club, manager of tea shop, Parkinson's research at local med school, Local Scholarship Award x4, NYS Seal of Biliteracy in French, NYS Seal of Biliteracy in Latin
Major: Neuroscience

ESSAY

Why Tea Does Not Belong in Tea Bags

A seed is planted in the ground. It grows tall and fast into a rich, succulent plant on the jagged yet gentle mountain slopes of Yunnan, China. A young woman plucks a leaf from the plant, and a journey begins. The tea has been born.

I encourage you to drink a cup of tea as you read. Hold it close to your bosom and feel its warmth. But as you put the tea away, be prepared to look at it differently when you reach for it again.

As the freshly plucked tea leaves are carried from high in the mountains, the fresh and grassy scent of the plant washes over the mountain top. The basket meanders through the bushes to a tea factory. So begins the magic; or in some cases, a tragedy.

The leaves begin by resting in the sun; they lay out to develop in the therapeutic heat of Spring. As the light and warmth of this first season of life rush into them, each leaf gains the sweetness and flexible forgiveness of a young child. Its journey has begun and as each leaf is rolled by hand, the artisan has only added character and strength to each leaf. A caring and supportive cooperative of tea producers can create the difference between a bitter beverage, and a sweet, melodic sip.

The aforementioned tragedy begins as the leaves, having been so kindly treated, depart from their mother factory and into their adolescence. The harsh world will meet the leaves—so optimistic and gleeful—to challenge every molecule of their delicate composition.

This cruel world that seeks to take full advantage of the poor leaves may be named Lipton. The self-interested and indulgent Lipton will take the well cared for leaves and bully them into dust; taking a whole, strong, elastic leaf and crushing it into mere ash. Here in their adolescence, these leaves' futures are truly tested. The gleeful brightness that fled the leaves in production now struggles to surface in the cup.

Now, you may be cradling your cup of tea right now, or thinking fondly of the tea bags sitting in your cupboard, questioning this claim that tea does not belong in tea bags. But tea, just like people, can be healed and grow stronger from injustices done to them in the past.

Tea became an important part of my life when I began frequenting a local tea shop. Through this global, loving culture I met people and learned skills that would help save me from the betrayals and strife that foreshadowed my future. I liken my life to that of tea leaves. I was treated with love in my childhood: I had an easy life full of joy and hope. I thrived in school and at home and knew that it would last forever.

A bomb dropped. When I was thirteen, my mother passed

away from colon cancer, and my father turned to the bottle. I was left alone to take care of my dog and my brother one week before my freshman year of high school. I was crushed into dust and, on my own, was forced to redeem a character that might overshadow the bitter taste.

Of course, the challenges never ceased. I face challenges every day, but this experience forced me to appreciate the beautiful years that I did have; it showed me to redeem everything I could that was left in my soul, and to fight for the future I knew I would have. Although I didn't come from a thriving tea bush in the mountains of Yunnan, I did come from a thriving home in the clutches of my beautiful mother, and my family at the tea shop has filled the gaps left behind. Their love has helped me renew my strength, and has therein renewed the shiny potential I was gifted.

REVIEW

What did the essay do well?

Kyra begins her essay with a beautiful tale of the tea leaves, ending the story of the tea's journey with the argument that tea leaves do not belong in tea bags. The application of tea as a beautiful creation of several different obstacles that yields both the bitter and a sweet sip in a warm drink effectively transitions into Kyra's challenges at home. Kyra's essay did a great job of combining two seemingly unrelated topics into a powerful reflection of her own growth. Kyra parallels the interesting narrative experience of the tea bag and its injustices to losing her mother and how that loss changed her family and the family dynamics. Ending her essay with gratitude and appreciation for her past is an integral structural component of the essay. Doing so allows the reader to see why these events matter and showcases Kyra's source of strength to brace future challenges.

What could be improved about the essay?

While the essay's lyrical tale of the tea leaves' journey is well executed, the transition to Kyra's family life could use more storytelling, as it is rather abrupt. In addition to connecting the tea leaves' injustices and perseverance to her own life, Kyra can add more examples of how she overcame obstacles after her mother's passing. Adding more concrete details would allow the reader to be more grounded back into what the essay is truly about, Kyra.

What made this essay memorable?

The essay was memorable because it was written in a very beautiful and poetic way without coming across as forced. Rather, it was sophisticated in its plot and descriptive, metaphorical ability. Additionally, the effective execution of the metaphor and its attention-grabbing bottom line "tea does not belong in tea bags" allowed the reader to leave with a strong impression of the story and its underlying message.

—Linda Lin

Simon L.

Hometown: Hacienda Heights, California, USA
High School: Public school, 500 students in graduating class
GPA: 3.9 out of 4.0 (4.5 Weighted)
SAT/ACT: undisclosed
Extracurriculars and Awards: IB and AP, USA Swimming National Team
Major: Human Evolutionary Biology

ESSAY

On January 18, 2013, a strident voice bellowed over the school's loudspeaker, "Simon L—: Please come up to attendance." I nonchalantly packed my backpack and meandered over to the attendance office. I noticed my father and a close family friend conferring with my middle school principal. I immediately detected the palpable anxiety and tension. My knees start shaking, and my skin's pallor repelled the eyes of those around me. With hesitation, my father and our friend held my hand and walked me to the car, where grim news inevitably awaited.

"Listen, Nene. Mami had a heart attack."

In a trembling voice, I asked if she was alive. He quickly reassured me that she was. I was silent all the way to the hospital.

Gelid air flew through the hospital corridors, foreshadowing a life-changing moment. As I hastened to the ICU unit, anxiety rushed through my body. The constant, aggravating beeping of medical machines and the doctors' apprehensive whispers portended hopelessness. My mother was surrounded by tubes and machines: I was overwhelmed. I stared blankly at the ceiling, searching for hope. I mustered the strength to tell her about my day and that I loved her, ignorant that this would be the last time I would ever speak with my mom. Thirty minutes later as I prepared at home for swim practice, my father informed me that my mother had passed away from Hodgkin's Lymphoma. I dropped my bag in shock and ran into his arms, tears rushing down my face.

Challenging? A word that does not do this event justice.

Her death was a shock to me as my father had previously shared nothing about my mother's condition. I was angry with him because he thought by shielding me from her condition he "protected" me. Ironically, this decision split our relationship apart. I no longer trusted him. I internalized my anger, my sadness, and my confusion.

I dreaded attending classes. I was heartbroken when she didn't pick me up from school just like every other day. I distanced myself from my peers to avoid their questions. My teachers appeared indifferent toward my loss.

My mother's death also hindered my performance in the sport I loved: swimming. The day after her death, I swam one of the best races of my life in her honor. But after that, I began missing practices. Staring constantly at a black line on the bottom of the pool exacerbated my grief. My goggles hid my tears, but they could not hide my despondency. The pool changed from being a beloved sanctuary into a cemetery for my thoughts.

As recently as my junior year, I battled bouts of depression, but, with counseling, grit, and grace, I have transformed into a strong, young adult. I now train and swim in my mother's honor. Her initials grace my swim cap, and her spiritual presence provides tenacity that is unwavering and authentic.

My dad and I have developed an open and earnest relationship.

Learning to communicate openly without my mother as a bridge and facilitator has made us closer after the initial abyss. He attends all my meets, whether they are the World Championships in Budapest, Hungary; Junior Nationals in Austin, Texas; or high school meets in La Habra, California.

I now possess a new respect for a mother's role and her dedication to providing the best life for her child. Many children fail to appreciate their mother's ubiquitous presence or acknowledge their endless devotion.

The rigor of academia—which initially was another challenge after my tragedy—has become a source of both refuge and inspiration. I am eager to continue to develop as a scholar at the university level, and my original intent of studying medicine has developed a profound meaning. Armed with resiliency, empathy, and humility, I will never again be the scared and unsuspecting child that was called up to the office that day.

REVIEW

What did the essay do well?

The opening sentences hook the reader into a high-stakes moment, expertly setting the scene for the devastation that is to come. The narration that follows gracefully illustrates the author's resilience and ability to overcome a devastating life event and also repurpose it as fuel for navigating future challenges. Through candidly describing the adverse day-to-day toll that the death had on the author, the essay becomes more personal and powerful. A satisfying conclusion ties the essay together and ushers in a sense of the story coming full circle, reminding readers of how his strength of mind is here to stay.

What could be improved about the essay?

The second half of the essay, where the author focuses on the ramifications for his personal life, could elaborate more on how his loss motivated his academic interests and shaped him into the person he is today. He could dive deeper into how his values and outlook on life truly shifted by citing more personal anecdotes. "Show, don't tell," one of the principles of immersive writing that helps the reader step into the shoes of the character, is key for demonstrating the evolution of his character traits. The writing should delineate his transformation into his own person—for instance, instead of blatantly stating that the father-son relationship has improved, the author could reframe his closeness with his father in a way that unveils something more about how he prioritizes familial intimacy and communication over all else.

What made this essay memorable?

It painted an incredible picture of how he emerged stronger from something that no child should have to endure—the loss of a parent—with patience and fortitude, fighting to mentally stay afloat while training to become a world-class athlete. The essay was structured well and naturally transitioned from one instance to another, which created an easy to follow, yet impactful, narrative.

—Libby Wu

MICHAEL T.

Hometown: Newark, New Jersey, USA
High School: Public charter school, 144 students in graduating class
GPA: 4.05 out of 4.0 (4.56 Weighted)
SAT: 1390
Extracurriculars and Awards: President of high school speech team, Governor's award in Art Education, IT and Customer Engagement intern at Audible Inc., volunteer at National Speech and Debate Association, publicist for National Honor Society, tutored middle school students, AP Language and Composition tutor, Algebra II tutor, International Thespian Society, forum leader/advisory leader
Major: Sociology

ESSAY

I've been alone for three years now.

My freshman year, my mother had to take a job as a live-in caregiver to make enough money to pay rent and other bills after my uncle got married and moved out. I was ecstatic. I could finally have the entire house to myself. I had imagined the countless hours on the PS4, nobody telling me to go to sleep or to go do my homework. I felt free. Unexpectedly, though, this freedom came at the expense of my childhood.

To compensate for never being home, my mother called me three times a day. The first call would always be at 6:00 a.m., like clockwork. That was the call to wake me up so that I wouldn't miss the bus and be late for school. Then there was the 4:00 p.m. call where we went over anything and everything that happened in school that day. Lastly, there was the 7:00 p.m. call which always seemed to last over an hour. This was the call that made me miss my mother the most. We labeled this call the "multi-purpose" call. Sometimes we would just talk about how we were both doing. Other times she would teach me things I needed to know, like how to do laundry, how to go grocery shopping, or how to cook. But one thing that she always seemed to bring up was how she wished things were different and how much she ached with the desire to be home with her son.

That last call always weighed heavily on my heart. When around friends and their families, I would often put my head down and smile because their interactions would remind me so much of when my mother was with me every day. It made me miss her insurmountably, to the point where I began to despise every aspect of this "independence." To me, it was loneliness, isolation, and nights laying in bed wishing I had a loved one in the house that I could talk to or hug. I was forced to become a man instead of living out my days as a kid. What hurt me the most, though, was knowing that my mother hated our situation even more than I did. She hated knowing her only child was growing up without her and it hurt her more than words could explain. She would always say how I was her pride and joy, but I've always thought of myself to be her hope, her hope for a better life.

That is why I have worked so hard in school. My mother has dedicated and sacrificed years of her life to make sure that her son could live a great one, and all she has ever asked from me in return was to do well in school. There were numerous times when I felt discouraged and unmotivated, but the thought of letting down the woman that has broken her back for me was far stronger than any fatigue I may have felt.

For three long years now, I have entered my house after school expecting nothing but silence and darkness. I lay in bed at night yearning to hear any sound at all that would signal that there was life in the house beside me. Then I wake up the next morning, get ready for school, and start the cycle all over again. I have almost gotten used to being alone. But I won't let my story end here. The reason why I have worked myself so hard is so that things can be different for me and my mother. She always says that everything she's doing now is for me and that when she gets old it'll be my turn. Except when my turn comes, she will never have to be alone.

REVIEW

What did the essay do well?

Overall, this essay was very powerful. The author establishes a situation that is extremely unique, and really has a solid grasp on how it affected him, especially as a high school senior. His perspective of having all this freedom is the classic dream of every high school student. However, his realization of what the situation actually entails establishes a deeper understanding of his situation.

Furthermore, there is a clear outline of how Michael has grown and developed based on his experiences, and all of it culminates in his final sentence: "Except when my turn comes, she will never have to be alone." This is both a powerful and effective closing statement that sums up the ideals of the entire essay.

What could be improved about the essay?

Although the essay was very powerful, there are some structural changes that could help clarify the author's points. This essay was powerful and carefully written; however, the second and third paragraphs are quite long and appear as a "wall of text," which could be a drag on the readers. Even including an extra line break or two, as well as including more specific quotes if possible, would allow the reader to swallow what Michael has written, consuming all the information provided.

What made this essay memorable?

The conclusion of this essay was extremely memorable. Each sentence is like another whirlwind of emotion, giving the reader a taste of what Michael has experienced all over again. It's like telling the story all over again, but changing the expected ending. It's a clear indication of change, as the parallels of the situation show his growth and are a way to lay out what qualities he's exemplifying clearly and obviously. The purpose and execution of the concluding paragraph make it and the entire essay memorable.

—Matthew Sheridan

LISBER G.M.

Hometown: Philadelphia, Pennsylvania, USA
High School: Public school, 200 students in graduating class
GPA: 3.97 out of 4.0
SAT: 1480
Extracurriculars and Awards: Bowling, poetry slam, softball, High Honors
Major: Computer Science

ESSAY

"And lastly . . ."

My name was not called. I didn't make the volleyball team. At that moment, I thought about the last hour and three months that I spent giving this tryout my best effort, only to be rejected. This was the start of my sophomore year.

The previous summer, I'd decided that I wanted to become a leader to give back to my community and maybe even gain the undeniable confidence my mother has. It seemed that leadership only had two routes: to serve on the counsel of a club or join a sport, like my mother had. However, I had failed at both.

But before I had a chance to attempt again, my family and I had to move in with friends in Pennsylvania due to a home eviction. I was still motivated to become confident and seek leadership, but didn't know where to start. My Chemistry teacher, with whom I shared my hobbies writing poetry, informed me of the new poetry slam club starting that year. I was reluctant to visit the club at first. I feared public speaking would once again expose me to the judgmental looks I received when I couldn't speak English. Still, my curiosity got the best of me and soon I was standing at the door.

I felt intimidated being surrounded by people reciting poems. Poetry before seemed gentle, but the members sought to make political statements with their work and recitation—full of history and iconic figures. Moreover, they exuded the confidence I lacked. The next club day, I asked my coach to "teach me the 'swag.'" I explained the "swag" meant performing in a way that demanded attention. That "swag" made poetry electric, and I wanted to explore and wield that side of poetry.

But first, I had to admit that I had only been mimicking poems I'd seen, but nothing personal to me. I began to brainstorm new ideas every day, only to realize the common theme was my mom. For so long, I watched how my mom personified tenacity as she worked hard to pay the bills while researching ways to fulfill her dream of becoming a nurse. Before I knew it, I found my new path to my "swag": to relay the love and passion I learned through watching my mother.

In a month, I stood alone on the stage, shaking with anticipation and anxiety. My verses were clear in my mind, but I could hear my voice tremble and then my thoughts stopped completely. Still, I pushed through my performance. By the end, I stood immobile and self-conscious. Then I heard snapping. I looked up to see judges nodding and right beside them my coach, moved to tears.

Each performance after that came with so much more ease because I was confident that I belonged on that stage. I didn't need the title of captain to be a leader. Simply being involved in something I'm passionate about, and having the confidence to share it with others, is leadership.

REVIEW

What did the essay do well?

This essay takes its readers on a roller coaster of emotions from the get-go. The introductory quote sets the stage for a sports-based narrative. The reader is meant to think it's the typical story of someone not making the sports team and trying hard the next time and making it, but this essay is not that. Instead, Lisber decides to use a sports hook to set the reader up for some excitement. She then transitions into using the unique experience of a home eviction to talk about her tenacious and dedicated mother as well as how the mother's personality is a model for hers.

The imagery of the poetry slam, including all the relatable emotions of anxiety, fear, and eventually confidence, is all enveloped perfectly by the emotions surrounding her home eviction as well as the mother chasing a similar dream (of finding her way).

What could be improved about the essay?

The overall structure of the essay could use some adjustment to improve it. It's the typical story of "I need this quality, but I can't get it in this typical way so I need to go outside my comfort zone." Luckily, the emotion and imagery provided in the essay as well as the unique story of Lisber all help to add to the power of her message, as well as exemplify what hurdles she needed to overcome to not only possess leadership but also have a unique spin on it.

What made this essay memorable?

What really made this memorable was the tie-in of Lisber's mother's experiences with her own. Lisber described how they both went through the same eviction and had struggles, so showing that they were "in this together" and similarly overcame struggles helped Lisber's admissions case.

—Matthew Sheridan

Haley S.

Hometown: Portland, Maine, USA
High School: Public school, 180 students in graduating class
GPA: 3.8 out of 4.0 (3.99 Weighted)
SAT/ACT: undisclosed
Extracurriculars and Awards: Theater, speech and debate, keynote speaker at assemblies and support groups and on radio and TV across New England, newspaper, film society, Poetry Club, Greater Portland Youth Poetry, Poetry Nation's National Amateur Poetry Competition Semi-Finalist, Falmouth School Board representative, work as a waitress, teacher, and camp counselor, Gay Straight Trans Alliance
Major: Economics and Psychology

ESSAY

An exceptional pain struck my right shoulder just hours after a routine track practice. I reported the symptoms to my father who promptly administered Tylenol. While adjusting myself restlessly on our living room sofa, the sharp sensation rapidly spread across my body. For a fleeting moment, all my muscles tightened and trapped me in utter agony. Then, ninety seconds passed and a release overwhelmed me. I was completely paralyzed.

At twelve, I suffered a rare spinal cord stroke which left me entirely immobile and unfeeling yet still cognitively intact. While lying in the coffin-like chamber of a five-hour MRI, I vividly recall evaluating my future. In the natural order of adolescent priority, I wondered if I would return home in time for school the next morning. Frantic doctors strung my unmoving limbs through countless inconclusive examinations: a spinal tap, angiogram, CT scan, and three MRIs would diagnose me with a stroke a neurologist claimed he had never encountered and hoped to never encounter again.

Baffled doctors revealed to my parents that I would be forever paralyzed, unable to breathe on my own. They recommended the immediate and permanent attachment of a ventilator. In a defiant, desperate attempt to save my life, I was transferred to a Boston hospital. Throughout the course of the transfer, I contracted pneumonia, sepsis, and eventually septic shock. My deteriorating conditions rendered my survival nothing short of miraculous.

My hunger was satisfied by the dispensing of a glucose and water concoction through feeding tubes. Excruciating sensations pierced my shoulder, ironically indicating the onset of recovery. Recovery would be accompanied by discouraging setbacks, mental torment, and a major dependency on nurses. Regardless of the circumstances, I chose to maintain a positive outlook.

I was graciously blanketed with optimism from my community. I began inpatient rehabilitation after eleven days in intensive care. I ritualistically engaged in physical, occupational, and speech therapies for a near fifty days of rehab. Despite medical odds, I reclaimed the ability to breathe, eat, and talk without assistance.

I escaped the confines of my hospital bed and eventually the limits of a wheelchair. At the end of my inpatient stay at Spaulding Rehabilitation Hospital, I limped beyond the entrance with a walker. Even with substantial weakness on my right side requiring years of outpatient therapy, I relished my triumph.

My residual deficits include minor sensation weakness on my right side and the inability to move my right hand. The remaining physical damage from my stroke is nonetheless incomparable to the fortune and privilege I have obtained. I have been gifted insight into the strength of humanity. Particularly, I have witnessed raw, uncensored battles between life-threatening illness and innocent children; I have witnessed courage in its truest form. After my battle, I feel wholeheartedly responsible to use my recovered being as a vessel to serve the families on the pediatric floors of my hospitals. I published a memoir recounting the stages of my stroke and have donated the proceeds. I have worked tirelessly to transform societal discomfort with disabilities through writing and public speaking. Ultimately, I have overcome.

I am unfamiliar with the young athlete who I was before my injury, yet I yearn for a chance to talk to her. Upon greeting her, I would extend a lifeless hand. Sensitive to how little time she has with her health, I would speak unhesitatingly. I would prepare her briefly, gently, withholding the impending pain and uncertainty.

Then, after reveling in her potential, I'd demand she sprint away from me.

I would watch as she hurries from our conversation. Although her fear may leave her breathless, she does not suffocate; she will conquer great strides in denser air. She will clear tremendous hurdles and fill bleachers with spectators who will cherish her victories. She is young and unknowing now, but I am the living proof that she will find her way.

REVIEW

What did the essay do well?

Haley begins her essay with a vivid traumatic moment that immediately captures the reader's attention. As she guides us through her essay using a descriptive tone, she allows us to vicariously experience her trauma and her ultimate path to recovery. Her carefully articulated sentences do an excellent job of showing the reader the extent and impact of this moment in Haley's life. Additionally, it allows us to better understand her circumstance while garnering empathy from the readers. While what happened to Haley is very unfortunate, she ultimately learned more about herself, her community, and her past, while demonstrating growth and overcoming a significant challenge.

What could be improved about the essay?

While Haley's journey of recovery must have been painful, I wished she would have elaborated more on what she has taken away from this experience and how she has applied what she has learned in this experience to other aspects of her life. I would have loved it if rather than lumping everything together towards the end, Haley had written more about the mental torment and emotional battles that she has described throughout the course of her hospital stay. To me, the ending felt like an attempt to wrap up a well-detailed description of her challenge, and I would have loved to see this message echoed earlier throughout the essay, in order to provide a clearer transition between the events and her takeaways.

What made this essay memorable?

The rich contextualization as well as the descriptions keep the readers focused. Haley takes us through her journey in the hospital, and this helps Haley amass empathy from the readers, as we are cheering for her successes and sharing her frustration during her setbacks. The powerful narrative elicits attention from the readers, which makes this one of the more memorable essays that I have read.

—Truong Nguyen

GRED B.

Hometown: Durres, Albania
High School: Private school, 100 students in graduating class
GPA: 10 out of 10
SAT: 1520
Extracurriculars and Awards: Bronze medal in MYMC, Performance with Distinction in Canadian Open Mathematical Challenge, winner of the Second Prize in the National Mathematical Olympiad, winner of the Third Prize in the National Biology Olympiad, winner of the First Prize in the National Mathematical Olympiad, participant in Junior Balkan Mathematical Olympiad, delegate in European Youth Parliament ARNISA 2018, winner of Science Olympiads-Durres (2nd phase), the main character of several school plays, gold medal Winner in 3-Minute Science Short Movie, volunteer guide in the Amphitheater of Durres, activist in Red Cross, Udhëtim i Lirë, CSDS, Shpresa, member of student government, guitarist in different local shows, captain of the volleyball team
Major: Computer Science and Mathematics

ESSAY

"Let my wooden guitar vent."

"Fire!"

I rubbed my eyes again. But the fire was still there.

The fire reflected in my eyes had invaded the depths of my soul. My classical guitar "Toledo" stood there silent, motionless . . . among my beloved things, which not only didn't help me, but they collected pieces from my past and challenged hardheadedly the bitter reality inside and out. The math workbooks crashed into the ground. Was math really worth it?! The right triangle was not right. The irrational number not acting rational. The problems were fictional and they always had a solution. Would my problems have a solution too? I felt my breathing . . . the only proof of the present, holding tight to it, the past would not come again and the future . . . unknown. My hands suddenly, took the guitar.

"I'm sorry, son . . . but, I was fired today . . ." the chords G, Am, F

"Mom is tired, let her rest . . ." G, Am, F . . .

I was playing my favorite song "Don't you worry child." Was I playing it because I liked it or to escape the reality?!

"Don't you worry . . ." I kept repeating to myself, unable to say this to my restless parents.

The guitar had taken control of me. The notes collided with each other, fought, struggled to find the "key." As I sought to take control, they counterattacked me with the only question: "Why me?" And how could I negotiate with "Why me?" It was invincible. In these two words lay all the strength of the injustice of the Albanian system: the bureaucracy, the misguided politics and the harsh economic situation of the country. In these circumstances, my father had chosen to openly express his political beliefs. He wanted change, something some called stupidity and some bravery, especially for a state employee. I also wanted change, not knowing how or when. My dad got a termination letter.

"Money, power or fame?" is the question that is posed to every man with ambition. My mother would have chosen money for sure, since she was exhausted by that naughty thing which impinged the silence in our family. And I felt powerless. "Oh, I wish I had a strong hand, to punch the heart of the silent mountain!"—the verses of our poet, Migjeni, came to me.

Worn out, I left the guitar . . . I got on my knees . . . and prayed. I saw the situation and I realized where to start. I decided that I had to do something . . . not to change the old Gred, but my situation. I went out. Time was passing.

"Mom, I found a job!" I said entering the house, not prideful, but hopeful. I knew that the part-time job would not solve our problems, but I wanted to do something for my parents, because in all my successes, certificates and medals, they had done their share.

I woke up after a difficult night, when dreams received abstract colors and shapes. If these dreams hadn't surprised me enough, the next day, when I washed my eyes, I noticed that the fire was still there. This time, the lighting was different. It reflected hope, which was transmitted across my body, as the current in an electric guitar.

I realized that from this experience I had changed, I had grown up and become more responsible. The suffering had given me strength and vitality. The math workbooks were in place and the guitar . . . well, it would play a new explosive song this time, that of my life.

"Don't you worry, don't you worry child
See heaven's got a plan for you."

REVIEW

What did the essay do well?

The author leveraged many musical, academic, and cultural references to elucidate his appreciation for the arts and the aesthetics of life. The vivid imagery and strong storytelling demonstrate that he has a strong grasp of how the past and the present, the real and the imagined, can mesh together to make life both interesting and less daunting. Music anchors the progression of this story, as he uses it to frame how he processes his family's setback, which implies that he is well-rounded enough to be equipped with all the tools he needs in the face of future adversity. Furthermore, the author's use of fire imagery illustrates his ability to quickly adapt to tough situations, which is also seen by his noble sense of agency that motivates him to tackle any problem that arises. Finally, the ending seamlessly circles back to the beginning of the essay, evoking a sense of triumph and comfort in the reader.

What could be improved about the essay?

The meaning of the opening quote is a bit confusing, and it could have been less abruptly placed in the story. Also, instead of directly stating in the last few sentences that this experience accelerated his growth, the author could have demonstrated that through further use of metaphors or imagery. Although you want to stay within the word limit when writing your essay, you don't want the ending to feel rushed.

What made this essay memorable?

This piece truly showcased how emotionally mature and attentive he is to the needs of loved ones around him. The writer's unique use of punctuation creates a nontraditional structure that keeps the reader focused on what will happen next. The rather short sentences at the beginning of the essay set a fast-paced narrative that reflects the burning fire the author has described in relation to his musical journey. He is able to transcend personal fears to rise to the occasion and be a son his parents—and, most importantly, he himself—can be proud of.

—Libby Wu

Francisco M.

Hometown: Dallas, Texas, USA
High School: Public school, 96 students in graduating class
GPA: 3.7 out of 5.0 (4.35 Weighted)
SAT: 1470
Extracurriculars and Awards: National Hispanic Recognition Program, NSBE TMAL 1st place, 2nd place TAME Science Divisional, 5th place Science TAME State, 3rd place TAME Science Divisional
Major: Mechanical Engineering

ESSAY

Three days before I got on a plane to go across the country for six weeks I quit milk cold-turkey. I had gone to the chiropractor to get a general checkup. I knew I had scoliosis and other problems; however, I learned that because of my excessive, to say the least, intake of milk my body had developed a hormone imbalance. I decided it would be best for my health to completely stop drinking milk and avoid dairy when possible. Little did I know, this was only the start of a summer of change; three days later I got on a plane to attend the Minority Introduction To Engineering and Science (MITES) program in Massachusetts.

I assumed that most of the people were going to be unhealthily competitive because of my past experiences. I thought I would keep to myself, do my work, and come back no different. Living in a building with 80 people I've never met in a place I've never been while making a significant lifestyle change was not easy. The first few days were not kind: I got mild stomach ulcers, it was awkward, and I felt out of place. That first Thursday night, however, all of that started to change. On Thursday evenings we had "Family Meetings" and on this particular Thursday part of our Machine Learning class was working together when the time came to go to the dining hall for whatever this "Family Meeting" was. Honestly, we dreaded it at first, "I have work to do" was the most common phrase. We learned that "Family Meeting" was a safe space for us to talk about anything and everything. Today's theme was, "what's something important about your identity that makes you unique?," but the conversation quickly evolved into so much more. People spoke about losing family members, being shunned at home, not feeling comfortable in their own skin, and more. So many people opened up about incredibly personal things, I felt honored to be given that trust. The room was somber and warm with empathy as the meeting concluded. Out of my peripheral vision I saw Izzy, one of my Machine Learning classmates, rushing back to the conference room. I realized something was not right. Instinctively, I followed her back to where we were working. Izzy sat down and immediately broke down, the rest of us filed in as she started to talk about what was wrong. It felt as though an ambulance was sitting on my chest, my breaths were short and stingy. I was afraid; afraid my support wouldn't be good enough, afraid to show that I cared, afraid they didn't care for me. In this one moment all my insecurities, some I didn't even know I had, came to the surface. The heavy silence of hushed sobbing was broken by an outpouring of support and a hug. We all started sharing what we're going through and even some of our past trauma. Slowly that weight is lifted off my chest. I feel comfortable, I feel wanted, I feel safe.

This is the first time I truly felt confident, empowered, and loved. I am surrounded by people smarter than me and I don't feel any lesser because of it. I have become the true Francisco, or Cisco as they call me. I now, at all times, am unapologetically myself. The difference is night and day. As the program progressed I only felt more comfortable and safe, enough so to even go up and speak at a family meeting. These people, this family, treated me right. I gained priceless confidence, social skills, self-worth, empathetic ability, and mental fortitude to take with me and grow on for the rest of my life. Through all of this somehow cutting out the biggest part of my diet became the least impactful part of my summer.

REVIEW

What did the essay do well?

Francisco's essay comes across as very genuine and easy to read. Being overly verbose is a common mistake students make when trying too hard to use sophisticated vocabulary and instead makes their writing hard to understand. He avoids this by writing with clarity while showcasing his growth over the course of an experience. The growth Francisco shows and the detailed examples he uses when describing his experience at the MITES program highlight his strengths as a student, and his confidence in learning and connecting with others is useful in showing application readers how he would contribute as a student at their institution.

What could be improved about the essay?

The structure of this essay could be improved. The three large paragraphs into which the essay is divided make it more difficult to follow at times. Francisco could organize his ideas into more groups, making it easier for readers to follow the subject and purpose of each paragraph in the essay. Additionally, the opening topic of the author's struggle with scoliosis and his attempt to regulate it is not touched upon again until the very end of the essay, which makes it seem less relevant to the rest of the essay's subjects. Intertwining the topic of scoliosis more frequently throughout the essay will help remind the reader of Francisco's journey and showcase a more cohesive narrative.

What made this essay memorable?

What stands out about Francisco after reading this essay is his ability to contribute positively to a learning environment through the impressive experience of the MITES program, which he describes. Francisco alternates between the challenges in this new environment and his raw emotions, which grounds the reader in the essay. There is also a great sense of his personal qualities that make him not only a valuable student but also someone who has grown and is willing to connect with and encourage others, contributing to the vibrant social environment at Harvard.

—Isabella Tran

ASHLEY F.

Hometown: Clarence Center, New York, USA
High School: Private school, 63 students in graduating class
GPA: 4.0 out of 4.0 (Weighted)
SAT/ACT: undisclosed
Extracurriculars and Awards: National Honor Society, Mock Trial, student government, a cappella group, school newspaper, literary magazine
Major: Government and Art, Film & Visual Studies

ESSAY

I am a hobbit—a tiny creature with abnormally large and extremely hairy feet who enjoys eating second breakfasts with my hobbit family. I reside in my little hobbit hole in the peaceful Shire where nothing dangerous or adventurous ever happens. But just like Bilbo Baggins, I embarked on an unexpected journey of my own one day, finding my courage not in a dark cave inhabited by Gollum, but in high school as a timid freshman who soon learned the value of self-confidence.

It all started when I decided to participate in Mock Trial, a club where students are given a fictional case to try in front of a judge in a courtroom. I was interested in learning more about what a career in law would entail, so I thought it would be wise to gain some experience. Some may scoff at the idea of a tiny hobbit working in a law firm, trying cases in courtrooms, but I had never allowed anyone to make me feel like I couldn't do something, and I wasn't going to start now. The only person who ever hindered me was myself, and my fear of failure, or "messing up," often led me to doubt my abilities and refuse to try something new. With Mock Trial, I knew I was pushing my limits.

Our team consisted of only six participants, so in order to compete in the trials, we would have to act as both lawyers and witnesses. My shy, unadventurous hobbit-self urged me to quit, to give up and take the easy road home to enjoy third, or perhaps even fourth breakfasts. It assured me that if I quit, I wouldn't have to worry about losing, about failing and disappointing myself. But my experience in high school had shown me that I didn't have to be perfect. I wasn't going to get a perfect score on every test, and I wasn't going to answer every question correctly, but I was still going to try. All I had to be was myself, and if I could get over my fear of failure, I could have the courage to continue trying.

I refused to give up easily, so in the weeks leading up to the trial, my teammates and I worked tirelessly to prepare our questions and our witnesses for direct and cross examinations. We stayed after school every day and met with our club moderator for suggestions and advice during study halls. Even though I was the only hobbit, I enjoyed working with my teammates. In the end, our preparation paid off, and we won our first trial. I was proud of what my teammates and I had accomplished together. If we had lost the trial, we still wouldn't have failed because we gained valuable experience that day.

Now, years later, I'm interested in pursuing a career in biomedical research to develop treatments for diseases. The invaluable skills I gained from Mock Trial will continue to be relevant as I move into college and explore career options in the medical field. It has shown me that self-reliance is the key to unlocking the doors of opportunity: if I have the courage to try something new, I will always have the chance to broaden my knowledge.

This past summer, I participated in the Young Scientist Research Program at Canisius College and I was able to speak with many doctors about their research and contributions to the scientific community. During this two week program, I performed experiments and analyzed the data to form conclusions. I wouldn't have had the fortitude to participate in a summer program had I not pushed myself freshman year and joined Mock Trial. I can now visualize myself as a miniature hobbit with a pristine lab coat, working in a lab to develop cures . . . something I never thought would have been possible just a few years ago.

REVIEW

What did the essay do well?

Ashley writes a strong essay recounting an instance of challenging herself to join her high school Mock Trial team. At the same time, she characterizes herself as a hobbit who lives in a safe place "where nothing dangerous or adventurous ever happens." As her essay develops, Ashley mentions her hesitation to join the team, citing her shyness and fear of failure. However, she manages to deliver the meaningful message that by getting over her fear and working hard alongside her teammates, she had a successful first trial and gained a new perspective by trying something new. Finally, Ashley connects this past experience to her future aspirations as a biomedical researcher. She asserts that her Mock Trial experience showed her that "self-reliance is the key to unlocking the doors of opportunity," and this reflection highlights her growth in approaching her ambitions with confidence rather than reservation.

What could be improved about the essay?

Although Ashley flexes her creative muscles by incorporating the hobbit metaphor into her essay, there are certain cases in which this comparison feels out of place in her narrative. Her story is a relatable and naturally interesting one, but at times she interrupted her story with a misplaced hobbit reference. For example, her mentioning that "even though I was the only hobbit, I enjoyed working with my teammates" does not add to the narrative and instead serves to distract the reader from her otherwise meaningful experience. Making sure to reference this metaphor more sparingly would have immersed the reader more deeply in her essay.

What made this essay memorable?

Ashley differentiates her essay by weaving the creative hobbit motif into her personal story, and she enhances her essay's message by doing so. An admissions officer reading her essay would be immediately more interested in the story she has to tell because of this decision.

—Daniel Berk

III.
INTELLECTUAL
DESIRES

KIRAN A.

Hometown: Long Island, New York, USA
High School: Public school, 410 students in graduating class
GPA: 103.65 out of 100
SAT/ACT: undisclosed
Extracurriculars and Awards: Science Research, Mathletes, Science Olympiad, National Honor Society, Science Technology Engineering Program, National AP Scholar, LISC Best in Chemistry Award, Junior Science and Humanities Symposium (JSHS)
Major: Electrical Engineering

ESSAY

I was never a reader, nor did I like English class until my teacher handed me a dusty, color-faded book titled *The Catcher in the Rye*. I know, "never judge a book by its cover," but nothing interested me about that book. No light bulb clicked, and no "aha" moment happened. Throughout high school, I've been very STEM-oriented, so I didn't expect much from a book. However, with every flipping of the page, my curiosity about the cause of Holden Caulfield's behavior sparked. I wanted to understand the root of his mental instability. Soon, I couldn't put the book down. I had to know why. I began researching the book and found there was a prequel to it that would be published in 2060. I could hardly wait until English class for our book discussion every day, and this prequel was asking me to wait 40 years? Never more did I wish that there was a way in which I could time travel.

I had to find an answer to feed my curiosity, so I contacted Princeton University, the place where the unpublished prequel sits. After a few days of emailing, asking if I may visit to view the work, I bought a train ticket and traveled on my own—something that I had never done before—to read the prequel. On the four-hour journey to Princeton, I contemplated how I never thought I'd find myself on a train for a book. In between switching trains from NY to NJ transit, I thought to myself, "Am I really doing this?" But I didn't turn back. As I sat in the secured space of the Princeton library, I reflected on how this book changed my entire perspective on literature and how through it, I've learned that I have an interest for coming-of-age literature. This genre reveals the harsh truth of society, which is that oftentimes, there are no great endings.

Not only did I find the answer to the question that I kept in my mind for weeks, but I also found the answer to what I may want to do in college and what I want in my "dream school." This book helped me discover my interest in social sciences. We use the phrase "this isn't rocket science" to depict effortless tasks, but that's very misleading. As computer scientist Duncan Watts said, we associate difficulty with sciences such as astrophysics, but NASA has launched hundreds of rockets; difficulty should be associated with social sciences. We spend years studying the brain but are still unable to predict human behavior. Neuroscience is a marriage between psychology and biology, and for now, it's the closest we can get to mind-reading and predicting behavior.

After leaving Princeton that day, I emailed my English teacher and shared my newfound knowledge with him. When I returned to school, he told me that in all his years of teaching, no student had ever embarked on an intellectual experience like I had. As a result of that one book, I became a student who surpasses the thresholds of the classroom and now searches for more topics that push conversations beyond classroom discussions. When applying to college, I looked for a college that values that same concept—intellectual exploration—over anything else: a place where I would be surrounded by people who are not only like-minded, but also open-minded.

I've missed out on community in high school. Having multiple interests and minority backgrounds, making friends was challenging because some aspect of me would always stand out. That's where Harvard fits in. At Harvard, learning doesn't stop once you leave the classroom. Whether it's discussing culture with others in the South Asian Women's Collective, making friendships with people of common background through Harvard Undergraduate PRIMUS, engaging in summer research through the PRISE program, or joining one of various book clubs, Harvard screams intellectual exploration and community. Furthermore, at Harvard, I can pursue interdisciplinary interests. I can take STEM classes while simultaneously being immersed in South Asian literature studies in Dr. Asani's class. I don't want to give up any of my interests—STEM, literature, or social sciences—and at Harvard, I won't have to.

REVIEW

What did the essay do well?

The author starts by acknowledging a weakness rather than identifying a strength—not being interested in reading. This approach not only is creative but also allows Kiran to showcase a different side to her interests that could otherwise not be found in her application. While her extracurriculars or classes might indicate an interest in STEM, this essay highlights a different aspect of her life, but with equally great passion for this intellectual experience despite not usually gravitating towards literature. This is the best use of a personal essay—to convey aspects of your identity that may otherwise go unnoticed.

The essay also has great organization and very clear writing. The authorial voice comes across as genuine, and the details of the experience show a real passion for learning and a great example of exploring curiosity.

What could be improved about the essay?

The final paragraph of the essay is very specific to Harvard and can probably be changed if the author planned on reusing this essay for other colleges. That itself is not a bad thing, but the fact that the final paragraph feels tacked on and disconnected to the rest of the essay makes it seem less impactful in the end. The conclusion to an essay is important because final words are what stick with readers more than any other part of the essay, so it is important to use them to leave a long-lasting impression of you as a person.

What made this essay memorable?

The topic itself is a unique experience that shows off the author's dedication to intellectual pursuits. Not many people would go out of their way to satisfy curiosity, but that is a great quality that universities are looking for in potential students. The premise of the not-yet-published prequel provides a sense of excitement about the unknown, even to the reader.

—Isabella Tran

Harry G.

Hometown: Cherry Hill, New Jersey, USA
High School: Public school, 547 students in graduating class
GPA: 3.8 out of 4.0 (6.7 Weighted)
SAT: 1550
Extracurriculars and Awards: Track and field (varsity, 2017–2018 Coach's Award), wrestling (junior varsity, 2018–2019 Cougar Award), school newspaper editor (National Scholastic Press Association Superior Award in Ethics Writing), High School Hall of Fame, Dwight D. Eisenhower Leadership Award, cum laude
Major: Integrative Biology

ESSAY
"Tuyo"

Mid–Atlantic Ocean, en route to Rome, Italy. It's 3:46 a.m. Eastern, 9:46 a.m. local time. From the airline seat pocket in front of me, over the roar of two turbofan engines and the general bustle in the cabin, I become aware that my phone's alarm had sounded. As I shrugged off the shroud of sleep I hear those words I've heard so many times before: "Soy el fuego que arde tu piel" (I'm the fire that burns your skin). It is the opening line to "Tuyo," the theme song from Netflix's *Narcos*. Once I'm fully awake, I notice several passengers seated in front and to the side of me, looking on in surprise and annoyance. My younger brother eyes me murderously. He and my fellow passengers have been listening to Rodrigo Amarante's Colombian bolero more than 15 minutes. Sheepishly, I shut off the alarm, remove the airline-issued sleeping mask from my forehead, and begin to listen to former Navy SEAL David Goggins's "Can't Hurt Me" on Audible. Why, you might ask, do I have my phone primed to blare the *Narcos* theme song at 3:30 a.m., even while on vacation with my family? I'd love to tell you that my original reasons were deeply rooted in my desire for personal discipline and efficiency—waking up early so that I can exercise, get ahead in homework or even simply read a book for pleasure. The origins of my alarm ritual were far less stirring. My first experiences setting an early alarm began in sixth grade after I received my first phone. As an eleven-year-old, being able to wake up before daylight introduced me to a new world—the world between 3:30 and 6 a.m. The world, reposed in dark and quiet, was without distraction, stress or worry. I felt at peace. This soon became my time, and I filled it with my own simple pleasures, like watching the news or catching up with my favorite podcasts. Eventually, after committing to learning Spanish, I changed the alarm to the *Narcos* theme song. Now, I haven't done the research, but I'm fairly certain I'm the only person at 3:30 a.m. on the east coast learning the *Narcos* theme song. Nevertheless, and despite your likely incredulity, the *Narcos* theme song provided me the opportunity to work on something difficult, but ultimately fulfilling.

Beyond memorizing the lyrics to "Tuyo" and other Spanish songs, I have had to resolve more serious difficulties in my life; namely, reconciling the lack of congruence between my inherent interest in the "hard" sciences and my natural talents, which align more with the "soft" sciences. More personally, I possess my dad's talents but my mom's goals. My dad is a clinical psychologist and former English major, a man comfortable in the world of words. My mother, a nurse practitioner whose doctoral thesis involved standardizing care for individuals suffering from acute head injuries, is definitively the hard scientist of the two. While my mother sends me links to articles about new studies on how various foods can affect our genes, my father recommends I read every novel written by Pat Conroy. While my parents are situated comfortably within their own talents and interests, I sometimes feel less certain. Proficiency in Mathematics, Engineering and Physics have not always come easily. Perhaps it is because I have been surrounded by scientists my entire life that I have longed for a career in the sciences. Since childhood, the doctors, astronomers and engineers in my own family showed me how science can make a tangible difference in the world. That is why I volunteered as a camp counselor at the Franklin Institute, a local science museum devoted to scientific education and research. While I spent far too many hours that summer chasing seven-year-olds through exhibits and de-escalating blood feuds over reportedly "rare" Lego pieces, I was encouraged by each child's burgeoning scientific curiosity. Seeing students' eyes, alight with curiosity as I guided them through activities involving planetary science and structural engineering, reminded me of my own childhood passions.

Though my childhood passion never waned, as I entered adolescence a new dimension in my view of a career in STEM emerged. If I'm being honest, there are not many people who look like me in the hard sciences. I'm of mixed-race, Caucasian, African and Cuban. Early on, I became inspired by accomplished scientists of color including Dr. Neil deGrasse Tyson, Dr. Mae Jemison and Dr. Ben Carson. Despite their circumstances, each achieved overwhelming success through hard work and commitment. In time, my inspiration turned to near infatuation. I began to benignly stalk Dr. Tyson. I wrote him letters, talked about his work to whomever would listen, and even dressed as him for Halloween (spending Halloween one year explaining to everyone the subject of my costume).

Eventually, I convinced my dad to take me to one of Dr. Tyson's lectures. The night of the lecture I brought a letter with me, sure that I would have a chance to meet my idol. Given the thousands of audience members, I did not meet him that night. My fanboy status, however, remained intact. At the risk of prompting a restraining order on behalf of Dr. Tyson, I hereby acknowledge that between the ages of 11 and 15, there was a young stalker out there watching his every move. I wish I could say that I completely outgrew that phase. While I haven't dressed up as an astrophysicist in awhile (or stalked one, for that matter), my passion for science and scientists remains.

Over the years, in submitting myself to a pre-dawn ritual, I developed a code of personal discipline. By the time I turned 17, I had been following my routine for more than six years. It served as a constant reminder to put my best foot forward every day, even if that first step was just the one out of bed. Over time, my emerging self discipline began to play dividends. My Spanish continued to improve. I began to excel in my science endeavors. My SAT practice scores increased. I learned to enjoy new challenges. In time, I added new alarms to my wake-up playlist. Fancying myself a true innovator, I learned how to lower the volume so as not to disturb my family's sleeping schedule (most of the time, at least). My successes reassured me that my natural talents did not preclude me from one day achieving my goals. I was accepted into Johns Hopkins' Center for Talented Youth, where I studied astronomy and ethics at Roger Williams University and Dickinson College. Last year, I won the Naval Science Award at the Delaware Valley Science Fair for an engineering project. These served as further encouragement that I could pursue a career in the sciences.

Fortunately, exploring my passion for science hasn't prevented me from exploring my more dad-like talents. Since my sophomore year, I have been an editor of my high school's national-award winning newspaper, *Eastside*. There, I write opinion pieces and help other writers effectively communicate their views with the written word. This year, an opinion piece I wrote on gun culture in the United States was selected as a finalist by the Garden State Scholastic Press Association. I have found time to read novels, including one from my father's favorite author, Pat Conroy. While I have found success in the sciences, I have learned that I do not have to sacrifice the other part of me. In my high school classes and beyond, I have also seen more people who look like me. Perhaps the lesson is, never discount the power of a simple pre-dawn ritual to serve as a reminder to be better. For, as the *Narcos* theme song "Tuyo" promises in its title, whatever you want and are willing to work for will eventually be yours.

(PS: Just as a note to my future roommates: You can trust that I will not be waking you up at 3:30 a.m. I promise. I've got it under control.)

REVIEW

What did the essay do well?

Harry crafts an engaging narrative that touches upon many aspects of his life, from his early wake-up habits to his interest in STEM. He successfully portrays himself as a multifaceted individual who has a love for learning and self-betterment through personal anecdotes. In his opening, Harry hooks the reader by mentioning his tendency to wake up very early in the morning in an interesting way and opposes this with a personal struggle of his conflicting academic interests. He portrays these in an interesting light by describing them as mom talents versus "dad-like talents." Harry then combines these thoughts to portray a compelling picture of his identity. His essay leaves the reader with the lesson that channeling one's habits in a positive and constructive way can be a strong force for self-improvement.

What could be improved about the essay?

A quick fix that could improve the essay is some grammatical editing. His essay is marked by several small mistakes such as "awhile" or "play dividends" that interrupt the flow of the essay. Additionally, Harry's final two paragraphs are very resume-like—information that the Admissions Committee could find in the application. The essay could have benefited from a conclusion that was more creative. Lastly, the essay is beyond the current word limit for a college admissions essay.

What made this essay memorable?

This essay was extremely relatable. Everyone can understand the struggle of being interested in something but not excelling in it. Harry's is a story of overcoming this obstacle through hard work and determination, managing to reach his dream of pursuing STEM as his main academic interest. An admissions officer reading this essay would certainly be impressed by Harry's sheer dedication to learning (and his "Tuyo" alarm), which this essay makes apparent. I particularly enjoyed Harry's final "PS" to his future roommate, a nice integration of humor that adds character to the conclusion.

—Daniel Berk

ABBY Y.

Hometown: Clovis, California, USA
High School: Public school, 615 students in graduating class
GPA: 4.0 out of 4.0 (4.75 Weighted)
SAT/ACT: undisclosed
Extracurriculars and Awards: Community Advocate Intern for tobacco control policy at Economic Opportunities Commission, clinical researcher at local teaching hospital, ASB/Class President, Sunday school teacher, Youth Director of California Youth Advocacy Network (state youth tobacco control organization)
Major: Special Concentration in Food Systems

ESSAY

Barreling through the hallowed, mahogany double doors, I was on a mission. I made a beeline for the back. Behold, a panoply of new prospects, each beckoning me to read them.

Every weekend, my father, my sister, and I make the pilgrimage to Book Mecca. The sensations one meets upon entering Barnes and Noble are unmatched. The aroma of coffee mingles with the crisp perfume of unopened books and the tinny music drifts from the ceiling speakers, coalescing with the clanking of the Cafe equipment, which is intermittently overcome by the barista's peppy voice on the PA system announcing the latest limited-edition dessert. Where else can one enjoy a triple-layer cheesecake among bookstacks? As Virginia Woolf says, "one cannot think well, love well, sleep well, if one has not dined well."

My family, however, dines on knowledge. To us, Barnes and

Noble is an all-you-can-eat buffet for the mind. After we snag our favorite corner table, I sit, like metal to a magnet, immovable for hours.

I may delve into an Agatha Christie novel and attempt to outwit Detective Poirot; though I never win, I find the sleuthing remarkably similar to analyzing confounders—the culprits of unexpected results—in my clinical research. Alternatively, I may crack open an atlas to test my memory from the summer when I memorized the entire world map. Or, I might read *Animal Farm* to better understand the system that ravaged Ethiopia in the late 20th century and forced my grandfather to flee his own village.

Complementing this mission to satisfy our voracious minds comes an equally important fulfillment: engaging with the coterie of miscellaneous characters we have befriended. After visiting the same Barnes and Noble for eleven years, we have forged friendships with several regulars, including a retired teacher couple, an octogenarian with a seven-year-old brother, and an eternally sunburned man named George who shelters feral cats at his pool company's office. After a dear Barnes and Noble–goer passed away, my heart was comforted when I read in her obituary that she, indeed, would be missed by "the old [bookstore] gang." United by their good humor and love for Barnes and Noble, this unlikely group teaches me that a community can form around anything, no matter how disparate the members are. They show me that, in Aristotle's words, "educating the mind without educating the heart is no education at all."

While I have the luxury of Barnes and Noble, my father's reality growing up in rural Ethiopia bears a stark contrast and defines my legacy of education. He received a meager education in a laughable schoolhouse, using sunlight to study by day, and the moonlight by night. When he was nine, my grandfather opened a school so my father could continue beyond 4th grade, unlike many of his peers.

My grandfather had no formal education, yet he knew the country's constitution by heart and exhorted nearby villages to educate their children.

My father's dedication to chauffeuring me to the bookstore and the library is an artifact of his father's same dedication. And I am the accumulation of this legacy. Behind me are all of the sacrifices and payoffs of my family's dedication to education, and before me is a lifetime of opportunity and fulfillment. Though I have never met my grandfather, I feel an incredibly palpable connection to him through our shared fervor to learn and teach. My father's and grandfather's stories remind me that education is not a commodity for many, but a privilege that I treat as such. I cherish all of my education's wonderful consequences: the obscure curiosities I have indulged in, the strong sense of identity I have developed, the discernment and morals I have bolstered, the respect I have gained for different viewpoints, and the ambition for excellence that I have inherited and extended. They are what fuel me, my college education, and my drive to pay it forward.

REVIEW

What did the essay do well?

Abby first hooks the reader by describing the journey to Barnes and Noble using terms such as "mission" and "pilgrimage," which are more commonly associated with much higher-stakes journeys and are incongruous with a casual trip to the store. Thus, the reader is left curious as to why these trips to Barnes and Noble are described in such a dramatic fashion and why Abby has such a strong connection to the store.

Throughout the essay Abby repeatedly highlights their

wide-ranging interests supported by the vast collection of Barnes and Noble. Through these references, Abby is able to demonstrate their curiosity for all subjects and their hunger for knowledge, which helps the reader to envision the sort of student that Abby will be at Harvard.

In the last half of the essay, Abby smoothly connects the more intellectual purposes of their Barnes and Noble visits to a discussion about the community that they found there as well as their own family's legacy of emphasizing education. In doing so they bring a more personal aspect to the essay and demonstrate their appreciation for and contribution to the communities that they are in.

What could be improved about the essay?

While likely used as a method to demonstrate the fact that they are well-read, Abby uses many colloquially uncommon words such as "panoply" and "coterie" that often distract from the flow of the essay and do not match the tone of the rest of the essay. While you want your essay to have a professional tone, it should not read like you are trying to come across as smart. Your intelligence will shine through without using overly complicated vocabulary.

What made this essay memorable?

Using the simple topic of Barnes and Noble, Abby produced a well-rounded essay that captured both their intellectual curiosities as well as their unique relationship with the Barnes and Noble community. Most people do not have such a deep attachment to a store or its people, so this essay especially highlights their ability to make connections through an intellectual journey.

—Amy X. Zhou

STEPHANIE B.

Hometown: Pompton Lakes, New Jersey, USA
High School: Public school, 150 students in graduating class
GPA: 4.07 out of 5.0 (4.83 Weighted)
ACT: 36
Extracurriculars and Awards: AP Scholar with Honors, National Hispanic Recognition Program, National Honor Society, Valedictorian, National Merit Commended Scholar, All County Honorable Mention for Discus, Class President, National Honor Society VP, Student Council VP, Track and Field Captain, Marching Band Drum Major, Health and Wellness Coalition President, Coalition of Student Ambassadors Secretary, Interact Volunteer Club President, Peer Helping, Tutoring, Panera Bread Cashier, Jazz Band, Concert Band, Chorus
Major: Art, Film & Visual Studies and Social Anthropology

ESSAY

In 1941, Argentinian author Jorge Luis Borges published a short story entitled "The Library of Babel" in which he chronicled a concept for a collection of every possible combination of 3,200 characters. In 2015, Jonathan Basile created a program that brought Borges' creation to life. A virtual library holding more books than atoms in the universe. Within these combinations of characters, by pure statistical probability lay every word, every phrase, every thought, and every idea; a hexagonal library of all possible existence within the bounds of human language.

In the now digital library lies the description of the universe's beginning as well as its end. Such circumstances would simply have to be found in the 10 to the power 4,677 books, each containing 410 pages within which lies every other possible outcome of the universe. However, the creation of this daunting feat creates an even more daunting perplexity: Is any human thought new or unique given that everything possible within our language is pre-recorded? Is it worth creating if everything already exists? Is it worth knowing if the truth is already there?

Many may say that knowledge is the purpose of life, however, I would like to contend that, as the acquisition of knowledge holds far more importance. We, as creatures who are capable of obtaining knowledge in mass, crave it. We are drawn to new information as a shark to a minnow. Yet we will never reach a point where we feel satisfied. We will never cease to explore for without such pursuit of wonder, we might as well cease to exist entirely.

Everyone finds themselves in their own pursuit of wonder beyond simply education. We wish to know the depth of the universe and count the species of beetles in the Amazon. We wish to know how to cook and how our loved ones are doing. We constantly take in information and surround ourselves with it. We want to read shelves of books and binge watch movies. We want to know about our planet and the people around us. We find interest in all the world has to offer and beyond.

While confined by the thought of the Library of Babel, it's important to remember the value in learning. The euphoria of discovery and the constant urge for improvement pushes humanity forward. In attending college, I want to find myself in an environment where the students and staff not only provide me with knowledge but support and further my pursuit of wonder along the way.

REVIEW

What did the essay do well?

Stephanie's essay provides a thought-provoking discussion of knowledge and the purpose of education. She dives into great detail about the Library of Babel, which fascinatingly holds more books than atoms in the universe. Stephanie then wrestles with the notion that human knowledge may not be creative or unique but rather the crystallization of a truth that already exists. Her conclusion, which centers on her realization that it is the process of acquiring knowledge that is meaningful, artfully brings together her essay's key themes while providing admissions officers a glimpse into the kind of student (and member of the Harvard community) that she will be. Beyond this, the essay effectively utilizes literary devices to highlight her writing abilities, something that admissions officers also consider when reading essays. The engaging story line combined with effective storytelling strategies makes for a very nicely crafted personal narrative.

What could be improved about the essay?

There could be a greater personal touch to the essay; it largely focuses on the Library of Babel and not Stephanie herself. Only two paragraphs mention how she fits into her analysis of learning—they could be expanded to discuss examples of how she has appreciated and will focus on the process of education. Less focus on the Library of Babel and more on Stephanie's experiences would provide stronger support for Stephanie's understanding of learning.

What made this essay memorable?

Stephanie travels quite well between a more philosophical discussion and applications to herself. She clearly contextualizes what the Library of Babel is and its connection to learning. I particularly enjoyed how, in her concluding remarks, Stephanie applied the ideas of her essay to the kind of student she will be at Harvard.

—Derek Chang

Nour K.

Hometown: McLean, Virginia, USA
High School: Public school, 493 students in graduating class
GPA: 3.873 out of 4.0 (4.343 Weighted)
ACT: 35
Extracurriculars and Awards: American Association of University Women Science Achievement Award, Georgetown University organic chemistry department intern, drum major of marching band, symphonic band, Smithsonian National Museum of Natural History Q?rius Youth Volunteer Gold Award, Model United Nations, jazz ensemble, McMatics Volunteer Tutoring Club, CheMnection Volunteer Tutoring Club, American Youth Symphonic Orchestra, McLeadership Student Mentor, National Merit Commended Scholar. Honor Societies: National, History, English, Tri-M Music, Mu Alpha Theta Math.
Major: Chemistry and Anthropology

ESSAY

A closed bathroom door. A frequent sight at the K. residence around 2004, yet not one driven by malicious intent, unless the use of toiletries is malicious. To four-year-old me, shampoos, conditioners, lotions, and anything else I found around the bathroom were best used for creating "potions." I spent hours upon hours giggling at the different colors and smells I could produce with what was available within a preschooler's arm's reach. Feeling the smooth mixtures squish between my fingers, swirling the orange juice pulp–like creations made by adding toilet paper to my potions, and watching the colors swirl down the drain were the most engaging parts of my simple childhood days. The happiness that came from my brief stint as a mad scientist–witch made my mother's scolding for clogging the sink with toilet paper just another part of the experience.

As I aged, I began to desire a new medium for my experiments. I turned away from the sink, walked down the hallway, out the door, and into the dirt in my backyard. It was here that I found my next subject for investigation: mud. Pies, figurines, bandages, you name it, and I could craft it out of mud. Its one-tone nature, different from my bathroom creations, did not disappoint me, as my interest was now captured by texture. Throughout elementary school, I delighted at the different consistencies I could create and rub along my arms and legs, again to the dismay of my mother, who was forced to bring towels and washcloths outside whenever my mud restaurant was open for business. I expanded my endeavors to the schoolyard, which had a garden perfect for my concoctions. There, I led my friends in discovering how unfamiliar types of dirt behaved, and creatively finding water sources to use for our merriment. I even began mixing peppers and herbs that had fallen off plants into the mud for a pop of color that made the restaurant idea all the more real. The frantic running that was necessary to wash the dirt off before class was the final element of adventure that ensured I returned for more every day.

Entering middle school signified a transition to a more school-centric life. No longer could I spend hours creating the mixtures that so pleased me, only for them to be washed down the drain. I curiously stuck my washed-free-of-mud hands into my mother's mixing bowl one day, and discovered a new discipline that I have continued with to this day, one that I know I can always fall back on whenever I desire. The feeling of eggs running through my fingers as I separate them, the sight of powdered sugar fluttering into the air as I mix it, and all other steps of a recipe provide me with the sensations I used to know from my mad scientist–witch and restaurant days. As I matured, I progressed from squandering bathroom products my parents had paid for, to harnessing the beauty of dirt after liberally applying water, to creating sweets for my whole family to enjoy. As I lost the blissful ignorance a child has of worldly matters like finances and resource conservation, my conscience was cleared by my discovery of a way to squish, squash, and mix until I created something delicious. The desire to feel something come to be in my own hands spread beyond the kitchen as I unconsciously realized that it could be satisfied in more ways than I would have ever thought. In constructing bookshelves, combining chemicals in labs, and crafting scale models, my need to create something from nothing is satisfied before I even notice it. As I continue to grow, I know that I will find a way to create something new in whatever I do, which is the true essence of magic that I was trying to capture in my potion-master days as a child.

REVIEW

What did the essay do well?

Throughout her essay, Nour uses excellent imagery and transitions to capture both her growth and her constant desire to create. She is able to find beauty in the ordinary and connect a theme throughout her different stages of life. Nour begins by describing her love of mixing toiletries together as a four-year-old, which evolved into mud-based experiments and has most recently turned into a passion for baking. This transition beautifully depicts her coming-of-age journey, as she progressed from toiletries to pastries, and in turn found herself in the various mediums she used to create. She wraps up the essay nicely with the realization that she loves working with her hands and applying herself from the lab to the workbench, illuminating the different ways she may choose to find intellectual stimulation at Harvard.

What could be improved about the essay?

Nour could expand on her present passion to create and how that contrasts with her earliest experimentation with toiletries—this could showcase some meaningful growth. Her paragraphs are also quite long, so the essay does not have as much structure to it as it could with more thoughtful partitioning. Additionally, some easy-to-fix grammatical errors bring down the quality of the piece. Proofreading to perfect grammar is a must for a successful essay.

What made this essay memorable?

This essay reveals everyday hobbies as indicative of a lifelong passion for creation. The unique evolution of Nour's creative journey—from toiletries to mudpies to bakery masterpieces—is a story that will linger in readers' minds, leaving a lasting impression from this creative and compelling narrative. The essay is very easy to understand and connects the author's different stages of life well together.

—Derek Chang

MANAS K.

Hometown: Pune, India
High School: Public school, 110 students in graduating class
GPA: 49 out of 52
SAT: 1530
Extracurriculars and Awards: Student council, sustainability, theater, Model UN, college tour guide, Outdoor Leadership, language immersion
Major: Economics and Government

ESSAY

I felt frustrated. The air of superiority UWC gave me over the locals of Dilijan—it didn't feel right and I knew it had to go. I had learned about the Sapir-Whorf hypothesis, the idea that a language shapes the way its speakers view the world. If I wanted to be able to see the world through the eyes of my Argentinian best friend, my Québécois roommate or the people of my host country, Armenia, I could only ever truly do so by speaking Spanish, French and Armenian. So, I decided to learn Armenian, the same way I had taught myself Spanish three years ago.

Armed with "Eastern Armenian for the English-speaking World" by Dora Sakayan, I stepped out of my little UWC bubble into the streets of Dilijan, where I met old babushkas who recounted endless stories of everything from their lives in the Soviet Union to the first time they fermented grapes. At first, their chronicles were elusive to me but after four months and hundreds of conversations, my nods turned into words. Everywhere I went, I met people who went out of their way for me simply because I spoke to them in their native tongue. Slowly but surely, this country was taking me in as one of its own.

To deepen my newfound love for its culture and language, I decided I'd spend my summer in Armenia. I studied linguistics and philosophy while staying with a host family, traveled to the unrecognized Republic of Nagorno-Karabakh, and tried my hand at beekeeping, all while hitchhiking. However, the most profound experience I had was mapping hiking trails for an ecological NGO in the south of Armenia. I had to map a terrain I did not know while accompanied by Armen, who could not see. Armen, the founder of the NGO, was completely blind but didn't allow his disability to stop him from connecting with nature. He insisted on coming on hikes with me and walked confidently behind me with one hand on my shoulder. Suddenly, speaking Armenian had changed from being a hobby to a responsibility. Every step brought with it more uncertainty and last-minute warnings from me. My accuracy in a language that wasn't even mine meant the difference between life and death for someone else. Fortunately, I was able to do justice to the trust he placed in me.

Learning to be his navigator was eye-opening in itself but it was my conversations with Armen that reminded me why I had chosen to leave home in the first place—to connect with a new culture and to learn from it. I realized that the priceless feeling of closeness, almost familial in nature, that developed over each hike was the solidarity my school was missing. Our multicultural yet isolated "bubble" rose impressively in the middle of a valley like a distinct mark of foreign power and influence. My peers and I conveniently blamed our inability to genuinely integrate with the community outside our campus gates on the language barrier and resigned to inaction and passivity.

Through my journey of learning Armenian while hiking in the Caucasus, I stopped viewing language as an impediment to the exchange of ideas. I learned to view it as an essential aspect of culture and even ensured that it became an integral part of my school's curriculum. And thanks to Armen and his unusually complex language, I went from living in United World College Dilijan to living in Dilijan, Armenia.

Where before I would have ignorantly seen chaos, I learned to see the true colors of Armenia; where some saw shanty houses, I now saw the humble homes where I was once invited for tea. And even though I'm leaving it soon, the love I have received from this land has made me realize that although I will never be Armenian by blood, I am Armenian by choice.

REVIEW

What did the essay do well?

This essay is a strong example of what a good narrative and structure looks like in a personal statement. The author opens the essay with an illustration of his setting and the paper's central theme: language. From there the author walks us through the importance of cultural exchange in his life while explaining how language can be the backdrop that can facilitate these changes. The particular strength in this narrative comes from how clear the concepts discussed in it relate to the author's life. His use of examples like meeting old babushkas who told war stories and spending a summer in Armenia helped bridge the gap between an abstract essay and their own personal story.

Another strength of this essay is the author's writing style. The author presents his ideas in a crystal clear and concise manner. This helps the reader make sense of a complex subject. Despite the conciseness, the writer is able to effectively communicate his emotions and passion for the subject through his writing, helping readers get a better sense of who he is as a person.

What could be improved about the essay?

While this essay was great, there are a few areas the author could have improved on. First, it would have been nice if he had provided a bit more context and details on the examples he provided. By including more parts of the conversation, the author would better solidify the importance of them.

What made this essay memorable?

This essay's shining star was the power of the narrative the author created. The purpose of a personal statement is to communicate who you are to a reader who has never met you. By his creating a narrative through such an interesting example, I was left feeling like I learned something new about life and about the author at the same time.

—Yab Demisie

Jailene R.

Hometown: Las Vegas, Nevada, USA
High School: Public school, 600 students in graduating class
GPA: 4.0 out of 4.0 (4.5 Weighted)
ACT: 32
Extracurriculars and Awards: Valedictorian, over 400 hours of volunteer work at hospital, founder of Friendly Faces student organization for students with special needs, Key Club president, honor society, ballet folklórico dancer, elementary school kindergarten teacher aide, QuestBridge Scholar, Hispanic Scholarship Fund Scholar
Major: Human Evolutionary Biology

ESSAY

"You'll understand when you're older." "You don't need to know now." "Shush, go play."

These were the slogans of my life, growing up. My unquenchable desire and desperation to know and understand everything became too much for my exhausted and overworked parents. They wished to help me, but they did not know how. No program or class I was enrolled in was ever enough. My curiosity towered over even the most qualified of teachers.

There are over 170,000 words in the English language, yet no word will ever be as crucial to my existence as the word why? An obsession with that three-letter word has fostered a passion within me, becoming a guiding light in a world of the wonderfully unknown, my brain always unsatisfied with simple Google answers and mediocre explanations.

When I was five, asking why was fundamental to understanding the small world in which I lived. Why were the colors named the way they were? Why was one plus two equal to three? My naivety fueled me because I wanted to know more, to understand more, but it drained my parents because they could not understand me enough to help.

When I was ten, asking why was fundamental to answering questions I could not begin to pose for fear of the repercussions of challenging my conservative and traditional family. All the same, these questions festered in the back of mind. Why did I have to believe in a god? Why did there have to be one? If a god truly loved us, why was my baby sister still in the hospital? Why was my father wading through pain and surgery because his efforts to provide for us risked his life and health? Why was it impossible to know everything in existence? Why did there have to be answers at all? I began to ask questions that would lead me to discover my passion for physics. Specifically, my love for astrophysics grew as I learned about the endless opportunities for questions and answers that exist within its realm.

When I was fifteen, asking why was fundamental to understanding the perilous world around me. Why did my immigrant mother potentially have to leave our country? Why was our family in danger of being torn apart when the only crime my mother ever committed was that of working for a better life? Why did I feel so empty and alone despite being surrounded by people every waking minute?

When I was sixteen, asking why was the weaponry I used to fight back against ignorance, stasis, and conformity. As my love for books grew, it was easier to find the answers I had so desperately yearned for. Why did I feel the way I did for other girls and not boys?

Why was I so bored in school? Why did I feel as if my parents did not know me, despite their raising me and giving me everything? Why did I feel happier outside of my own home?

Today, I do not know what asking why gives me. For every answer, I think of a hundred more questions. Why am I so different from my family? Why am I unable to be content with simple answers and mundane ideologies? Why have I always asked why? Why does questioning everything around me bring me calm and joy? Why can I not see the world as everyone around me does? I see it as a place where I can question everything, where I can be a true skeptic and question not only what I disagree with, or do not support, but, more importantly, what I do agree with and support.

While not everyone can appreciate the benefits of posing questions even when there are not always answers, for me, it is my liberation. Knowing that astrophysics embraces the unknown energizes me; it has forged my path.

REVIEW

What did the essay do well?

Jailene's essay begins with a reference to phrases almost every child remembers growing up, instantly creating a sense of nostalgia that maintains itself throughout the essay. This nostalgia creates a bond with the reader. Jailene tells a story of her life, describing aspects of her identity and personality through questions that begin with "why," tactfully revealing significant moments of her childhood such as struggling with her sexuality, facing her mother's immigration status, and conflicting with her parents. Her use of this question to guide her essay emphasizes her passion for the pursuit of discovery and suggests to admissions officers that she would pursue intellectual challenges at Harvard with enthusiasm and curiosity. Throughout the essay, Jailene intertwines her interests in an unusual explanation for her chosen concentration, presenting a multifaceted picture of her background and identity. The structure of the essay, composed almost entirely of questions, demonstrates a creative approach to the prompt and how Jailene might contribute to a college community.

What could be improved about the essay?

Jailene does an excellent job of revealing different parts of her personal life in this essay, but she could benefit from touching on how those experiences impacted her personally. She also could have described her personal interests in greater detail, focusing less on what happened to her and more on what she did as a result of those experiences.

What made this essay memorable?

Jailene combines beautiful prose and a touching story with a unique twist as she asks question after question that reveal her story. Using the question "Why?" as the central guide for the rest of her piece is as impactful as it is creative and unique. This accomplishes her delivery while playing on the motif of being denied answers, allowing Jailene to stand out among applicants for her skill with prose.

—Meredith Zielonka

Helen K.

Hometown: Oakton, Virginia, USA
High School: Public school, 540 students in graduating class
GPA: 4.0 out of 4.0 (4.633 Weighted)
SAT: 1570
Extracurriculars and Awards: Environmental movement to put solar panels on local schools, varsity debate, sailing instructor and race team, cross country, indoor track, spring track, environmental work restoring local brook trout fisheries with consistent data collection, math tutor of local students (donate profits to sports equipment for disadvantaged children), Rho Kappa Honor Society, National Honor Society, Math Honor Society, Harvard Prize Book Award, AP World History Award, French Award, Honors Biology Award, Science Fair (Plant Sciences) First Place
Major: Economics and Astrophysics

ESSAY

I wake up in monochrome. Just past the tips of my toes, the Flatiron Building rises above the bustling black and white streets of New York. Cars hurtle by in blurred gray tones. I am a hawk or helicopter or hot air balloon, and I have somehow worked myself into the sky of an Old Hollywood movie. Of course, this only lasts as long as I keep my eyes locked on the IKEA photograph I hung up across from my bed a few years back.

Just before I turned fourteen, I burst out of IKEA—my all-time favorite store—dead set on crafting on a "new and improved"

Helen. I rushed home, stripped my room, and launched my transformation. Out with the beaded golden comforter! Out with the floral rug! Out with the pastel prints of savanna animals!

Well, perhaps this is too dramatic. Items are rarely thrown out in the Krieger household, just put to another use. Gazelles and cheetahs now peer down at me from the hallway wall, and the floral carpet rests beneath the brass coffee table in the living room. As for the comforter, I still use the exact same one, just concealed by a stark white cover. Still, the meaning holds: I was ready to refocus. Life seemed to be accelerating and I was not going to sit by the roadside, watching the wheels kick up dust.

Back then, I did not know what I wanted to be, and I still do not know now. However, never has there been any doubt in my mind about what I want to be doing. I want to whiz from idea to idea, question to question, and all the while, learn as much as possible. In all its action of rushing cars, the IKEA photograph epitomizes this ambition. No billion-dollar skyscraper or jewelry store in New York could ever win me over. I am not after Gatsby's gilded highlife, but New York's dynamic—the city's perpetual drive.

When I open my eyes, however, I am just as likely to wake up in a vibrant forest of green as I am to rise in the midst of charcoal city streets. Plants flourish on either side of my headboard. Vines of English ivy cascade down my bookcase, and a sentry palm fans out in front of my closet doors. New York reigns over one wall, but the other three are governed by nature.

This contrast did not always exist. Apart from the occasional bouquet, the Krieger household was void of vegetation until my sophomore year. One Saturday, my copper phytoremediation experiment made the breakfast table home to four groups of greenery. Over the next few months, I watched parts of my garden flourish, and then wilt, and then (remarkably) recover. Although all my plants were eventually reduced to a green juice of sorts for absorbance testing, they had started a revolution.

Soon after my experiment ended, I realized I missed my garden, and the plant invasion began. Today, my room harbors seventeen species, meshed into a diverse jungle. A few have even spilled out, taking up residence in the living room and kitchen. Just as I am captivated by the movement of the city, I admire the delicate hardiness of plants. Left untouched by humans, forests would cover most of the United States, and even in the midst of man-made destruction, many species still find a way to break through the cement.

In my room, plants and city streets share the stage. They do not battle, but exist in equilibrium, the gray with the green, urban acceleration in balance with the stability of nature. These worlds are not opposites. For all their differences, they share the energy of growth as well as the promise of regeneration and renewal. To thrive, I need not tear myself between manmade landscape and the natural environment; I need not pick between rapid action and natural growth.

I choose both.

REVIEW

What did the essay do well?

Helen's writing immediately stands out with plenty of creative flair and a strong authorial voice that inserts personality and vibrance into this essay. The author is very technically skilled: she uses a variety of forms of punctuation and highly detailed descriptive writing, which makes the essay very engaging. She also varies the length of her sentences throughout, which keeps the writing punchy and the essay exciting.

With this style, the essay at times resembles the type of writing associated with fiction novels as it is very story-like, which showcases Helen's strength in writing but also highlights an attention to detail that a reader may possess as well.

What could be improved about the essay?

There may be a slight overuse of the "I" pronoun, rendering the sound to be slightly repetitive, but this is a very small detail. However, with such polished writing it is something to be considered. Also, with the technique and style of writing being exhibited so much (though it illuminates the subjects of the essay) it also ends up taking much of the spotlight rather than the author's ideas about growth and change. In a successful college essay, it is important to find a balance between showcasing your writing ability and presenting a full picture of yourself and your identity.

What made this essay memorable?

The author's unique writing style and her well-developed writing skill are standouts in this essay. Despite uncertainty about a specific idea for her future, Helen still showcases a love of learning and a passion for her various interests: writing and reading, reinvention, design and aesthetics, and science. Her final line is a very effective conclusion of the ideas presented throughout the essay. It is this curiosity and excitement about learning that sticks with readers in addition to her undoubtedly strong writing skills.

—Isabella Tran

JINNA C.

Hometown: New York City, New York, USA
High School: Private school, 86 students in graduating class
GPA: 95.2 out of 100.0
SAT: 1570
Extracurriculars and Awards: Girls cross country captain, editor-in-chief of the student newspaper, admissions prefect, school-wide honors for best history essay, debate, science, Mandarin, and individual leadership
Major: History

ESSAY

It's terrifying how much we can get from Amazon nowadays: groceries, clothes, books, and crises of faith are all just a click away.

After Audible thanked me for listening to *The Most Dangerous Branch: Inside the Supreme Court's Assault on the Constitution* by David Kaplan and *The Brethren* by Bob Woodward and Scott Armstrong, I wanted to cry, scream, and march to Washington to shake answers from Chief Justice John Roberts.

My emotional whirlwind burst from the dichotomy between reality and my expectation of it. Growing up, I knew the judicial branch as the apolitical arbiter of constitutional law and the bias-blind defender of civil rights. With fear across the nation rising as fast as the global temperature, I was sure the best way to change the failing status quo was through the courts. I dreamed of becoming a lawyer to advocate for justice and to help my country prosper. My ambitions sprouted from the ideals of public service ingrained into me at school and at home, and my goal hinged only upon the judiciary's mandate to protect our freedoms. My dream was purposeful and straightforward.

But 37 hours of audiobook rewrote all my beliefs in the judicial branch.

The Supreme Court: apolitical arbiter and bias-blind defender? No. Rather: potentially politicized, petty, proud, and irrational. Partisan politics dance about the Justices' Conferences. The Constitution and personal biases govern rulings. Most rights supposedly afforded by the Constitution are interpretations, not explicit clauses, of it. For example, Chief Justice Warren Burger manipulated case assignments, so Justice Potter Stewart tattled on him to Woodward and Armstrong in retaliation. The right of the judiciary to strike down laws deemed unconstitutional is derived more from *Marbury v. Madison* than from Article Three. Justice Harry Blackmun based his majority opinion in *Roe v. Wade* on the rights of the doctor to practice. Stare decisis is optional, as is judicial restraint.

I felt sick. I had worshipped the courts as the perfect forum for change, always upholding truth, equality, and scholarship; I saw them as the eventual birthplace of solutions to gun regulation, climate crises, gerrymandering, immigration, and social inequality. I did not want to acknowledge courts could be anything but perfect.

Desperation drove me to keep listening, but with every new case I covered, the clearer it became that I had worshipped an impossibility. After finishing Jeffrey Toobin's *The Nine*, I finally admitted that, prior to these books, I had known nothing. Perhaps that epiphany should have terrified me, but it did quite the opposite.

It was liberating.

Socrates once wrote that true knowledge was in knowing that you know nothing. I couldn't agree more: once you know you've hit wisdom rock bottom, you can be reckless with your curiosity because you only have everything to gain.

Since that epiphany, I have been gleefully chasing infinity. Even if my capacity to learn is finite, my curiosity is not. The history of the courts, the ethics of judicial restraint, the politics of judging, the rhetoric of opinions, the intersectionality of all of the above and more . . . there is so much to explore.

For the record: I purchased those audiobooks on a whim. I was not looking for anything more than a fascinating nonfiction read. But they have plunged me into an exhilarating, all-consuming, fully unpredictable adventure, one that stretches back to our nation's founding and far into our future. While these books initially upset me by revealing the imperfections of the judicial branch, they showed me a whole undiscovered history and future at my fingertips. Rather than smothering my dreams of public service, they fanned the flames; now, my dream of public service is fueled by my passion to serve and to learn.

And I'm ready to chase it.

REVIEW

What did the essay do well?

This essay is very topical. The frustration with the Supreme Court is not lost on any reader, regardless of political affiliation. Jinna uses the Supreme Court to show many things: her willingness to draw her own conclusions after extensive research, her ability to write well, and why she hopes to go into public service. The way she journeys through her understanding of the courts and the meaning of education provides a compelling picture of Jinna's intellectual curiosity.

What could be improved about the essay?

Writing about inherently political topics has the potential to be dangerous. Lean too far in one direction and an admissions officer may have the wrong idea about your ability to consider multiple (or even just their) perspectives. Jinna uses evidence to support her claims, but even then, it's clear she leans liberal. Nonetheless, this is a worthwhile risk when done well.

The tone of the latter half of the essay is inquisitive and open, which helps lessen the rigidity of her takes. Even then, a more neutral political tone could be taken to make the essay more agreeable. In addition, there are some legal terms that a layperson may not be familiar with; it's important that an essay is accessible to all readers to prevent the writer from trying to "sound smart" as opposed to truly demonstrating their knowledge on a topic.

What made this essay memorable?

The reader is able to come away from this essay with a clear sense of Jinna's passions, who she is, her strength in writing and dedication to her pursuits. Ultimately, she highlights a lot of her qualities that are valuable in students, like the pursuit of knowledge. I particularly enjoyed her line "once you know you've hit wisdom rock bottom, you can be reckless with your curiosity because you only have everything to gain."

—Natalie Martin

MICHELLE B.

Hometown: Chicago, Illinois, USA
High School: Public school, 1000 students in graduating class
GPA: 4.0 out of 4.0 (4.73 Weighted)
SAT: 1580
Extracurriculars and Awards: HOSA (Future Health Professionals) International 1st place in Biomedical Laboratory Science, YoungArts winner in classical music, National Council of Teachers of English (NCTE) Achievement in Writing Award, Scholastic Art and Writing Awards Gold Medal, Biology Olympiad (co-president), HOSA (school chapter president), Tri-M Music Honor Society (co–vice president), peer tutor, music teaching assistant volunteer, orchestra (vice president, violist)
Major: Neuroscience

ESSAY

> FISH OUT OF WATER: idiom. a person who is in an unnatural
> environment; completely out of place.

When I was ten, my dad told me we were moving to somewhere called "Eely-noise." The screen flashed blue as he scrolled through 6000 miles of water on Google Earth to find our new home. Swipe, swipe, swipe, and there it was: Illinois, as I later learned.

Moving to America was like going from freshwater into saltwater. Not only did my mom complain that American food was too salty, but I was helplessly caught in an estuary of languages, swept by daunting tides of tenses, articles, and homonyms. It's not a surprise that I developed an intense, breathless kind of thirst for what I now realize is my voice and self-expression.

This made sense because the only background I had in English was "Konglish"—an unhealthy hybrid of Korean and English—and broken phrases I picked up from SpongeBob. As soon as I stepped into my first class in America, I realized the gravity of the situation: I had to resort to clumsy pantomimes, or what I euphemistically called body language, to convey the simplest messages. School became an unending game of Pictionary.

Amid the dizzying pool of vowels and phonemes and idioms (why does spilling beans end friendships?), the only thing that made sense was pictures and diagrams. Necessarily, I soon became interested in biology as its textbook had the highest picture-to-text ratio. Although I didn't understand all the ant-like captions, the colorful diagrams were enough to catch my illiterate attention: a green ball of chyme rolling down the digestive tract, the rotor of the ATP synthase spinning like a waterwheel. Biology drew me with its ELL-friendliness and never let go.

I later learned in biology that when a freshwater fish goes in saltwater, it osmoregulates—it drinks a lot of water and urinates less. This used to hold true for my school day, when I constantly chugged water to fill awkward silences and lubricate my tongue to form better vowels. This habit in turn became a test of English-speaking and bladder control: I constantly missed the timing to go to the bathroom by worrying about how to ask. The only times I could express myself were through my fingers, between the pages of Debussy and under my pencil tip. To fulfill my need for self-expression and communication, I took up classical music, visual art, and later, creative writing. To this day, I will never forget the ineffable excitement when I delivered a concerto, finished a sculpture, and found beautiful words that I could not pronounce. If biology helped me understand, art helped me be understood.

There's something human, empathetic, even redemptive about both art and biology. While they helped me reconcile with English and my new home, their power to connect and heal people is much bigger than my example alone. In college and beyond, I want to pay them forward, whether by dedicating myself to scientific research, performing in benefit concerts, or simply sharing the beauty of the arts. Sometimes, language feels slippery like fish on my tongue. But knowing that there are things that transcend language grounds and inspires me. English seeped into my tongue eventually, but I still pursue biology and arts with the same, perhaps universal, exigency and sincerity: to understand and to be understood.

Over the years, I have come to acknowledge and adore my inner fish, that confused, tongue-twisted, and home-sick ELL kid from the other side of the world, which will forever coexist within me. And I've forgiven English, although I still can't pronounce words like "rural," because it gifted me with new passions to look forward to every day. Now, when I see kids with the same breathless look that I used to have gasping for home water, Don't worry, I want to tell them.

You'll find your water.

REVIEW

What did the essay do well?

The author's personal arc was described perfectly, allowing for readers to effortlessly understand her struggles and successes. She writes her story in a way that is easy to comprehend, beginning with a conflict that leads to instances of resolution and finalizing the essay with many real-world implications. Through her descriptive techniques, any reader can accurately perceive the challenges that she faced and how she overcame and grew from them.

I appreciated how the author explained how her interests and passions guided her through difficult times of her life. Because of this, the essay is able to send a strong overarching message revolving around the idea of pursuing what you love. The author also spends an equal amount of time talking about her hardships as she does her triumphs. Finally, at the end of the essay, she calls back to the beginning, displaying a nice use of symmetric literature.

What could be improved about the essay?

There are times when the essay exhibits a somewhat choppy structure. Additionally, beginning the essay with a quote and definition is quite a risk. The author handles it well in this example, although some readers may find this approach cliché.

What made this essay memorable?

The challenges that her story consists of are extremely memorable. She is able to reveal to the audience the issues she has faced and what she has learned from these difficulties. The author places each reader into her own shoes, forcing people to understand the gravity of her challenges, making for a memorable read. Lastly, I loved how she was able to apply what she had learned in her biology class to what she was dealing with in real life, especially by using complex and academic diction with words such as "osmoregulates." This technique was unique, stood out, and was used effectively.

—Matthew Doctoroff

Amy Z.

Hometown: Fishkill, New York, USA
High School: Public school, 506 students in graduating class
GPA: 98.5 out of 100 (102.79 Weighted)
ACT: 36
Extracurriculars and Awards: FBLA President, Science Olympiad president, debate, National Merit Scholar
Major: Computer Science and Government

ESSAY

There's a theory that even though each color has a specific wavelength that never changes, how people perceive a specific color may have subtle differences based on small differences in photoreceptors, and the color that one person might consider red might still be red in another's mind but could look different—a little duller, softer, cooler. Furthermore, how a person's brain processes the color may also be linked to that person's environment. Some studies have suggested that color sensitivity could be linked to one's native languages: for example, people who speak languages that have specific names for eleven colors are able to easily distinguish those eleven colors, but people who speak languages with fewer color specific words may have a harder time distinguishing them.

So it appears that even at the most elementary level of sight, the world is not an objective thing. Instead, what we know and what we remember can influence what and how we see. The color blue may just be the color blue to a three-year-old, perhaps her favorite color even, but an adult might connect it to so much more—the lake by his childhood home or the eye color of a loved one.

I first consciously became aware of the power that our experiences have to change perception when I went to turn on a light in my house after learning about photons in class. What had previously been a mundane light suddenly became a fascinating application of atomic structure, and I thought that I could almost perceive the electrons jumping up and down from energy level to energy level to produce the photons that I saw. I then realized that my world had steadily been changing throughout my years in school as I learned more and more. I now see oligopolies in the soda aisles of the supermarkets. I see the charges warring with each other in every strike of lightning, and the patterns of old American politics still swaying things today. Knowledge and making connections with that knowledge is the difference between seeing the seven oceans glittering in the sun and merely seeing the color blue. It's the difference between just seeing red and seeing the scarlet of roses blooming, the burgundy of blood pumping through veins, and crimson of anger so fierce that you could burst. Knowledge is color; it is depth, and it is seeing a whole new world without having to move an inch.

It is knowledge, too, that can bring people together. I love listening to people's stories and hearing about what they know and love, because if I learn about what they know, I can learn how they see the world; consequently, since behavior is often based upon perception, I can understand why a person behaves the way they do. On a road trip during the summer, my mom kept looking up at the streetlights lining the highways. When I asked why, she told me that whenever she saw lights by a highway she would wonder if her company had made them. She would guess how tall they were, how wide, and what style they were. She told me that ever since she started working for her company, lights no longer were just lights to her. They were a story of people who first had to measure the wind speed to figure out what dimension the lights had to be, and then of engineers, of money passing hands—possibly even under her own supervision as an accountant—and then of transportation, and of the people who had to install them. I might never perceive lights the exact way my mother does or see her "red" but by hearing her describe what she knows, I can understand her world and realize her role in ours.

Beauty and color are in the world, but it is seeking the unknown and making new connections that unlocks them from their greyscale cage.

REVIEW

What did the essay do well?

From the first sentence, Amy catches the reader's attention with a scientific theory. Amy uses this theory as a tool to discuss perspective, giving her the opportunity to showcase how she sees and understands the world and herself. This method of "showing, not telling," is powerful, engaging the reader far more than the basic statement of "everyone has a different perspective." Amy then describes how her own experiences affect her perspective. She uses a concrete example involving light: learning about photons. Amy's voice is particularly powerful in this paragraph, incorporating imagery to communicate how vivid her world has become.

In the fourth paragraph, Amy moves from observing herself to observing those around her, again using a concrete example of light: streetlights. Amy describes how her mother sees the world and communicates how, through her mother, she can recognize the importance of other points of view. In the first four paragraphs, Amy expands from looking at perspective as an isolated scientific concept to how she sees the world, and finally how other people see the world. Amy communicates in a single sentence at the end why perspective is important, thus executing a powerful conclusion.

What could be improved about the essay?

For the majority of Amy's essay, the structure is almost perfectly parallel. This structure, however, falters in the last sentence. It is not the stand-alone sentence that interferes, but the introduction of "seeking the unknown." While this final sentence is a valid conclusion from Amy's previous three paragraphs, the reader may fail to completely connect it back.

What made this essay memorable?

This essay is memorable because of how Amy uses the simple topic of color to describe how she sees and understands the entire world. If Amy can use her mind to find such meaning and significance in color, what else can she use it for?

—Helen Krieger

IV.
INFLUENTIAL
FIGURES

Jessica W.

Hometown: New Windsor, New York, USA
High School: Public school, 268 students in graduating class
GPA: 98.87 out of 100 (102.58 Weighted)
SAT: 1560
Extracurriculars and Awards: Valedictorian, National Merit Scholar, National AP Scholar, Poetry Out Loud NY state finalist, president of the National Honor Society, co-captain of the women's varsity tennis team, president of the female a cappella group, president of the Math Team
Major: Applied Mathematics

ESSAY

In my vision I focus on a lone front tooth backdropped by a black abyss; thin lips dance around it in motions forming words, yet I can't seem to hear them.

In the kitchen behind my grandfather sits his definition of luxury—a now stale and cold Filet-o-Fish from the Beijing McDonald's. American basketball plays on the television across from where we're sitting on the sofa; players' shoes squeak and balls bounce louder in my ears than those words. In this moment, his Mandarin goes in one ear and out the other. I don't listen the way I do when he's screaming at my mother, a bitter, blind rage fueled by undercurrents of fear and "I miss you."

My focus blurs, and the tooth disappears. Basketball fades to silence, and I'm on the airplane home to America. We're separated once more by an ocean and three thousand unspoken miles. It's a whirlwind; five years pass, and my few apathetic summers in China are over before I can blink twice.

The last clear memory I have is waking up on my thirteenth birthday to my dad handing me the landline kept for international phone calls: "Waigong has something he wants to read to you."

It is a poem that he had written about me. Through the phone, I could do nothing but hear his voice, static worsening the Mandarin already slurred by missing teeth. The poem says everything he loved about his granddaughter, everything he saw in her, despite barely knowing her. It is a reflection of last dreams, visions, and hopes of his own.

He was gone not long after that, once more turned to forever.

It wasn't until I found myself chancely entrenched in poetry because of a mandatory school competition that I began to think deeply about this disconnected relationship. Poetry Out Loud's anthology introduced me to hundreds and hundreds of poems, and I felt like a hungry child at a buffet. When I discovered "Old Men Playing Basketball" by B. H. Fairchild, I saw tired arms and shaky hands as a pure geometry of curves, hobbling slippers as the adamant remains of that old soft shoe of desire. In words, I was safe to miss my grandfather for all the things that made him human. For the first time in my life, I began to realize that I might have a love for beautiful words that ran deep in my blood, a love that couldn't be lost in translation.

On that makeshift podium in the school cafeteria my sophomore year, "Old Men Playing Basketball" becomes "Waigong Playing Basketball." I'm taken back to that sofa in Beijing one more time, where he takes my small hand into his tremoring one covered by gray-brown patches of melasma, where he tells me, "You are a gift, a wonder. You are a hu die." Butterfly: my Chinese name. Born to one day fly.

But it is no longer his voice I hear. It is my own—crisp and clear, raw and strong. The poem becomes the glass wand of autumn light breaking over the backboard, where boys rise up in old men. I see the whole scene this time, not just tooth and abyss. I hear every word.

Perhaps I will never be able to know my grandfather beyond his love of basketball and poetry, or hear his voice read me another poem. But when I am stirred by beautiful lines or liberated by my pen on paper, I know I am one of two same hearts, forever bound together by the permanence and power of language.

I am a vessel in flight, listening, writing, speaking to remember histories, to feel emotion, to carry forth dreams and visions and hopes of my own. My grandfather becomes an elegant mirage of a basketball player, carried by a quiet grace along my trail of spoken words floating upwards toward heaven.

REVIEW

What did the essay do well?

Though the essay is centered around the writer's grandfather, it manages to convey an extremely compelling, well-developed portrayal of the speaker herself. This is something that essays about another figure in your life should do well because although the subject may be someone else, the college application essay should ultimately aim to center and reveal information about yourself, not your subject, to the reader.

Through sensitive cultural juxtapositions and creative metaphors, the writer reveals her thoughtfulness, empathy, and clear artistic talent. The language is complex and emotionally resonant without coming across as overdone. Jessica manages to navigate transitions across significant physical and temporal distance particularly deftly in her third paragraph. The essay showcases narrative writing that is akin to what you might find in a novel, easily guiding the reader through the essay, making it easy to understand while also being sophisticated in style.

What could be improved about the essay?

Given the word limit of the Common Application, sacrificing some of the descriptive imagery of the speaker's grandfather to make room for concrete examples of her ability to embody a "vessel in flight" would have strengthened the overall narrative arc and pushed it forward. Examining the last paragraph in particular, what exactly has she listened to, spoken of, or written about? Certain adjectives and adverbs also seem redundant ("*chancely* entrenched," "think *deeply*"), increasing sentence length without altering the main point being communicated.

What made this essay memorable?

By grounding the reader in those deeply personal opening images of American basketball on TV and her grandfather's single tooth, Jessica avoids being constrained by a trite cliché and is instead able to develop her own sense of symbolism. She builds this up into an ending that holds just the right balance of wistfulness and closure.

—Cynthia Lu

LAUREN P.

Hometown: Olney, Maryland, USA
High School: Public school, 331 students in graduating class
GPA: 3.98 out of 4.0 (4.71 Weighted)
SAT/ACT: undisclosed
Extracurriculars and Awards: National policy director of Generation Ratify, Amnesty International National Inclusion, Diversity, Equality, and Accessibility member, co-creator and chief operating officer of InnovateX, policy director of Montgomery County Students for Change, debate captain of Poolesville High School debate team, Congressional intern for Congressman Jamie Raskin, Simon Wiesenthal Center digital terrorism researcher and analyst, The PeaceTech Lab digital terrorism researcher and analyst, Planned Parenthood DC Teen Council founder and teen educator, Take the Stage Performance Company Student Music Director, Amnesty International National Case Commitment Hero Award
Major: Government

ESSAY

Lunch and recess were opportunities to "play" Stephen Sondheim's *Sweeney Todd*, so we murdered our friends. We'd bake the dead into meat pies and scream cacophonously, "WE ALL DESERVE TO DIE!" Nine-year-old me even teased my hair, donned my Mrs. Lovett costume for Halloween, and rambled on about Australian penal colonies and how dead fiddle players make for "stringy" meat.

You cannot imagine my disappointment when everybody thought I was Frankenstein's Bride.

Like Gypsy Rose Lee, my siblings and I spent our formative years at rehearsals and performances, where I was indoctrinated into the cult that worships Sondheim. In our household, Sondheimian theater was a religion. (I'm not sure how I feel about God, but I do believe in Sondheim.) My brother and I read Sondheim's autobiography, *Finishing the Hat*, like the bible, reading the book cover to cover and returning to page one the moment we finished. At six, he introduced me to Sondheim's *West Side Story*, which illustrates the harms of poverty and systematic racism. Initially, I only appreciated Jerome Robbins' choreography (Sorry, Mr. Shakespeare). When I revisited the musical years later, I had a visceral reaction as I witnessed young adults engaging in deadly gang rivalries. Experiencing Tony's gruesome death forced me, a middle-class suburbanite, to feel the devastating effects of inner-city violence, and my belief in the need for early intervention programs to prevent urban gun violence was born.

I began to discover political and historical undertones in all of Sondheim's work. For example, *Assassins* whirlwinds from the Lincoln era up to Reagan's presidency. Originally, I simply thought it was hysterical to belt Lynette Fromme's love ballad to Charles Manson. Later, I realized how much history I had unknowingly retained from this musical. The song "November 22, 1963" reflects on America's most notorious assassination attempts, and alludes to each assassin being motivated by a desperate attempt to connect to a specific individual or culture to gain control over their life. *Assassins* awakened me to the flaws in some of our quintessential American ideals because the song "Everybody's Got the Right" illustrates how the American individualism enshrined in our Constitution can be twisted to support hate, harm, and entitlement. I internalized Sondheim's political commentary, and I see its relevance in America's most pressing issues. The misconstrued idea of limitless freedom can be detrimental to public health, worsening issues such as the climate crisis, gun violence, and the coronavirus pandemic. These existential threats largely stem from antiquated ideas that the rights of the few outweigh the rights of the majority. Ironically, a musical about individuals who tried to dismantle our American political system sparked my political interests, but this speaks to the power of Sondheim's music and my ability to make connections and draw inspiration from unlikely sources.

Absorbing historical and political commentary set to music allows my statistical and logical brain to better empathize with the characters, giving me a deeper understanding of the conflicts portrayed on stage, almost like reading a diary. Theatermakers are influenced by both history and their life experiences. I internalize their underlying themes and values, and my mindset shifts to reflect the art that I adore. I'm an aspiring political changemaker, and Sondheim's musicals influence my political opinions by enabling me to empathize with communities living drastically different lives from my own.

I sang Sondheim melodies before I could talk. As I grew intellectually and emotionally, Sondheim's musicals began to carry more weight. With each viewing, I retained new historical and political information. This ritual drives me to continue studying Sondheim and enables me to confidently walk my own path because Sondheim's work passively strengthens my ethics as I continue to extrapolate relevant life lessons from his melodies. Sondheim's stories, with their complex, morally ambiguous characters, have solidified my ironclad set of morals which, together with my love of history, have blossomed into a passion for human rights and politics.

REVIEW

What did the essay do well?

Lauren's essay showcases her personality and sharp wit as early as in the opening paragraph, which is the first of many jokes that she cracks. Comical references to musical theater and playful personal remarks are plentiful throughout the beginning paragraphs, which set the stage of Lauren's longtime interest in Sondheim. We also get to know a little about the author's relationship with her family through this interest, especially thanks to the metaphor comparing their household's worshipping of Sondheim to a cult or a religion. The author is able to address the essay's prompt well by providing insight into her quirky interests and allows her strong personality to resonate in her authorial voice.

What could be improved about the essay?

While the essay bridges the author's love of musical theater, and Sondheim in particular, to her passion for politics and social justice, this bridge can sometimes feel a bit forced. The issue seems to be the shift in the voice, which moves from being very goofy to much less quippy when discussing heavier topics. Especially since the first paragraphs contain a great number of details and witty remarks, the heavier tone in the second half, which does not replicate the exact same feeling, leaves that part of the essay less strong than the earlier paragraphs. Of course, when it comes to the topics of politics and human rights, you would not want to approach injustice with too much levity, but the voice could remain more consistent throughout the essay.

What made this essay memorable?

The essay's unique subject and the author's creative and humorous writing style strongly showcase many of her personal qualities. The essay paints a portrait of a very vibrant applicant whose humor, passion, and grit allow readers to have a strong sense of her personality.

—Isabella Tran

Ava B.

Hometown: Baldwin, New York, USA
High School: Public school, 350 students in graduating class
GPA: 97 out of 100 (115 Weighted)
SAT: 1540
Extracurriculars and Awards: Varsity volleyball, varsity lacrosse, National Honor Society president, Long Island Youth Orchestra, Wind Symphony president, Mathletes vice president, Athletes Helping Athletes, AIDS Peer Educators, Academons (trivia club), National Merit Scholarship Recognition, Harvard Book Award, Rensselaer Polytechnic Institute Scholarship, Volleyball All Class and Scholar Athlete, Tri-M Music Honors Society, class valedictorian
Major: Neuroscience

ESSAY

Some of my favorite moments with my dad are from the long car rides to volleyball tournaments across the East Coast. During the hours, he would tell me stories upon stories from his life. One of the most memorable is from when he was dating my mom. He and his parents did not speak for about a year because my mother is not Jewish and is black. This story led to my dad telling me how my mom did not even meet my grandparents until the reception after her wedding ceremony. As a 14-year-old, this was a shocking discovery.

When I was younger, I never noticed the differences in how my grandparents treated me and my two brothers as compared to my seven cousins. They went to all of my cousins' sporting events, yet only one game a season of my soccer games at the field less than five minutes from their house. They would also have a weekly dinner with each of my aunts, but not with my family. I was not old enough to understand, so I never felt that I was treated any differently.

My grandparents cannot be seen as entirely at fault with regards to our relationship. I have lived my whole life in the same town as them. My family could have put in more effort to see them. I went to a middle school that was minutes from their house yet never went over just to see them. There was a level of comfort that I did not feel because I was not close with my grandparents.

In the summer of 2015, I was going to sleep-away camp in New Hampshire. My grandmother had been battling cancer and before I left for camp, my dad told me that this goodbye to my grandmother could very well be my last one. While standing in a candy shop during parents weekend, my dad told me that grandmother had died. I stood for a few minutes with a mixture of shock and sadness. It did not feel like I had been able to appreciate the magnitude of losing a grandparent, someone I had known my entire life.

About a year later, my grandfather started dating Aida. From the first time that I met her, Aida was warm and welcoming. She immediately accepted my mixed-race family through her demands that my grandfather's house should have a wedding picture of my parents to complement the three other wedding pictures of my father's siblings. Aida treated me as one of her own grandchildren and I have never felt less than loved by her.

Now that I have a comparison between Aida and my grandmother, I realize that missing from my relationship with my grandmother was acceptance. I have a relationship with Aida in which we can do things together, just the two of us. When we are together, I feel that she is with me because she wants to be and not out of a sense of obligation.

I cherish the connection I have with Aida. I would like to have been close with my grandmother, but I am not going to regret that our relationship was not as full as it could have been. This failure stems from my grandmother's closed-mindedness and I prefer not to dwell on matters over which I have no control. I choose instead to rejoice in the love that I have in my life.

REVIEW

What did the essay do well?

Ava's essay touched beautifully on the vast spectrum of acceptance and nonacceptance within families: it reminds us that acceptance is sadly not something that can be taken for granted. Ava demonstrates a difficulty in her life experience centered around her mother's identity as well as her own in being black, but having that even impact your family experience is especially compounding. By writing about a figure who repaired this bond, Ava shifts the focus to be forward-looking and highlights her maturity in reflecting on acceptance.

Ava's use of short anecdotes throughout was effective in building out each relevant figure present in her piece, aiding in comparing and contrasting her experience with her grandmother and that with Aida. By including that Aida ensured Ava's parents' wedding photo stood on display next to her father's siblings', she conveys to the reader how important acceptance of her mixed-race family was to Aida, as compared to her grandparents.

What could be improved about the essay?

As strong as this essay is, it detracts focus from Ava herself. While Ava does not completely focus on other figures over herself, this essay could definitely be revised to put a stronger emphasis on her personal qualities and strengths that can be derived from this story. Qualities such as maturity, tolerance, and understanding are more implied than explicit, but the essay could benefit from adjusting that.

What made this essay memorable?

Ava tackles the difficult subject of familial acceptance of interracial marriages in a way that exhibits her warm character and focuses on the positives in her life rather than dwelling on what cannot be changed. She conveys a bittersweet emotion about her relationship with her grandmother with the powerful line, "It did not feel like I had been able to appreciate the magnitude of losing a grandparent, someone I had known my entire life."

—Kelly Kim

KELISHA W.

Hometown: Covington, Kentucky, USA
High School: Public school, 365 students in graduating class
GPA: 3.88 out of 4.0 (4.375 Weighted)
ACT: 32
Extracurriculars and Awards: Varsity track, Art Club, Leadership League, The Cougar Club, Junior Board, National Honor Society, youth mentor, Foster Youth Panel, Honor Roll, Integrity Pin, AP Scholar with Honors
Major: Psychology

ESSAY

I am a builder. No. I am a seasoned architect. My tools are foreign to the realities of others but mundane by my standards. I don't compose the perplexing and unique structures that most think of when the word architect is mentioned. Matter of fact, I don't make structures at all; my mastery is in the assembly of walls. Mental ones, to be exact. I am a skillful artist of intricately woven walls to create a complex maze for the others that try to get to know me; they are left confused, with no choice but to surrender their arbitrary efforts to "save" me.

I was unmatched in my array of skills. That was until I met Mark. Mark was a worker from my first mental hospital visits who had attached himself to my conscience before I could push him away as I had done with so many others. With an equally impressive skill set, he was able to navigate his way through my long-standing labyrinth to its center. That's where he found me. Still crouched next to my fledgling wall, dirt on my knees with dust on my face, I had finally been figured out for the first time in years. How did he get here? When did I let my guard down? The answers to these questions sat obnoxiously in front of me. The game that we always played. Horse. Such a benign game, that the thought of it having any significant part in my life is utterly incomprehensible. But it did, nonetheless.

Little did I know that Mark was studying to become a therapist in his studies of psychology, and I, his first patient. This is not a story of teenage love and life-changing heartbreak, but of one where an abandoned kid whose father raped her and whose mother gave up custody to have the father's perverted approval, finally gets the parental figure that she was never offered before. I was an emotional wreck at this time, not wanting to live, much less fight a court battle to get the "justice" everyone so badly wanted for me. So Mark, the father I never got to have, taught me how to swim in the never-ending circumstances I was drowning in. With every swish of the net of our game, a new way he would teach my fumbling feet to move in the water. And with every finished game, he was one wall closer to the reality behind my facade. He taught me that being angry at my circumstances would not fix them or get me any closer to overcoming them.

Nothing is going to change my mom's decision. Nothing is going to turn back time and change what my dad did. I can be the ruler of the lonely maze I created, or I can be surrounded by people who love and care for me. It wasn't easy destroying all the walls I had taken years to build and perfect, but it wasn't impossible either. This isn't a fairytale where Mark waved a magic wand and all was better and my walls disappeared from my mind. This is reality, and it took time, patience, and effort to unassemble my walls. Brick by painstaking brick. But in the actual world, people don't get happily ever after. Some of my walls are still there. And that's okay. I have learned to recognize my progress instead of singling out my flaws.

I am finally okay with not being perfect. My walls have chips and cracks, but I am content with their creation and their destruction. The destruction of familiarity is a beautiful thing. And so I climb out of the water, let the flowers bloom in the cracks of my walls, and walk off the court arm in arm with someone who sees me for who I am, not whom I pretend to be.

REVIEW

What did the essay do well?

Kelisha's essay, from introduction to conclusion, is very powerful, allowing readers to step into her world emotionally and experience her reality as someone who had to fight multiple battles from heartbreak to rape to a court battle for justice without the parental love she craved and needed. The writer utilizes a central anchor—her mental wall—to explain a unique ability to tune out the world. This introduces a theme that is further emphasized with the introduction of Mark, a future therapist, as someone who made an impact as a father figure that Kelisha desperately needed but never had. Mark allowed for a turning point and a time of reflection, building up Kelisha's resilience, confidence, and hope. By including Mark and his role in her development, Kelisha highlights the growth and change that she experienced from her struggle.

What could be improved about the essay?

Kelisha focuses on the cause of the building of a facade to hide past, sensitive experiences, and how she was finally able to recognize her true self and progress with the help of a psychology student. The essay would benefit from a deeper exploration of particular interactions between Kelisha and Mark that proved essential to her feeling more comfortable with herself and effectively deconstructing her walls.

What made this essay memorable?

The essay by itself, a personal narrative that delves into how Kelisha's past has shaped her, is memorable, but it is how Kelisha carefully crafts her prose that builds an emotional connection with the reader. The chronology of events, comparable to the effects on Kelisha's state of mind, allows readers to understand the writer's past and current state of being. This allows readers to fully grasp the impact of Mark and how Kelisha changed her perception of the world, being able to show her beautiful self without assembling more walls. Kelisha compares herself to an architect—one who constructs mental walls to protect herself from letting her guard down.

—Sophia Wang

CONNOR L.

Hometown: Gilford, New Hampshire, USA
High School: Public school, 120 students in graduating class
GPA: 4.0 out of 4.0 (4.7 Weighted)
SAT: 1570
Extracurriculars and Awards: Soccer, track and field, Unified basketball, volunteering
Major: Computer Science

ESSAY
Waking Up Early

Getting out of bed in the middle of a long, New Hampshire winter was never easy, but some mornings were especially difficult. On those particularly tough mornings, when the temperature could no longer be measured in the comfortable world of positive numbers, my dad would be up before the sun. He would turn on the gas fireplace in his bedroom, carry milk, cereal, bowls, and spoons upstairs, and then wake up me and my siblings. We would wrap ourselves in blankets as we ate our breakfast by the fire. I would complain about having to wake up early, never considering that my dad had been up long before.

Every morning for years he woke me up, packed my lunch, and drove me to school. He helped me with homework, coached my soccer team, and taught me how to ski. Even as I've gotten older and started to pour my own cereal, my dad hasn't stopped waking up early. He gets up long before my alarm clock even thinks about waking me, walks to his office (a desk, chair, and laptop situated above our garage), and starts to work. He works nearly every day, only taking the occasional break to engage in such leisure activities as splitting wood and mowing the lawn. As I've grown older I've looked up to him more and more.

There have been times in the past four years when I've come home with seemingly unbearable amounts of homework and I've thought, "I could settle for a B on this essay" or "How important really are the laws of thermodynamics?" On those late nights, when I'm on the verge of trading my notebooks in for a tv remote, I think about my dad. I think about how hard he's worked to make my life easier, and I realize that mediocrity isn't a viable option. I go downstairs, pour myself a glass of ice water, turn on some music, and get back to my work.

Sometimes it's hard to imagine my dad being young, but twenty-nine years ago, my dad was entering his senior year at Gilford High School. He had won a soccer championship under head coach Dave Pinkham, and was on track for another title that year. He was doing lawn care with his brother to make some extra money, and dreading the speech he would have to make at graduation.

I am now entering my senior year at Gilford High School. I won a soccer championship under the same Dave Pinkham as a sophomore, and hopefully I'm heading toward another this year. I'm running Leggett Lawn Care (which, despite its two unofficial part-time employees, has not yet gone public) and denying the inevitability of the speech I have to make this June. I'm keeping up my grades and trying to emulate my dad by putting others first. I teach Sunday School at my church, support the freshmen and sophomores on my soccer team, and give up countless hours of sleep helping my classmates with calculus. It's now my turn to go out into the world and figure out what I want to do and who I want to become. I don't know exactly where I see myself in five years; I don't even know which state I'll be living in next fall. I do know though that if I'm half the man my father is (which genetically I am), I'll have the strength and humility that I need to selflessly contribute to the world around me.

REVIEW

What did the essay do well?

The essay is very honest and describes the speaker's admiration for his role model, his father. It starts off with a seemingly mundane moment of waking up in the morning but then expands to talk about how he wishes to live up to his father's legacy. With straightforward prose, the writer illustrates the deeply emotional connection he has with his father. Reading the essay really feels like you are reading Connor's thoughts and that you are in his head as he goes through his morning. This level of clarity allows readers to connect instantly with the writer as they feel they are a part of him, experiencing the day as he does. The essay is able to portray this relationship in a moving way that also shows the writer's own drive and willingness to work hard.

What could be improved about the essay?

While I enjoyed reading this essay and was moved by it, I would hope for some more artistic or poetic elements. Including creative elements may have helped Connor create a more unique writing style that would help this essay stick out from others. While many of his essay's strengths lie in the direct, simple prose and I would advise against being overly verbose for the sake of trying to sound intelligent, being creative can be incorporated in a variety of ways.

Using a recurring motif or playing with more illustrative elements may make the essay more engaging for the reader.

What made this essay memorable?

This essay was able to tell the writer's story of his relationship with his father that many may be able to relate to. I, as the reader, not only was transported into the writer's world but also reflected on my own relationships with my family members.

—Amy R. Zhou

BRADLEY M.

Hometown: Gweru, Zimbabwe
High School: Private school, 100 students in graduating class
GPA: 4.0 out of 4.0
SAT: 1450
Extracurriculars and Awards: Chess, basketball, soccer, debate
Major: Economics

ESSAY

I woke up one morning to the usual noise in the kitchen. "That plate of porridge is mine," my brother yelled outrageously at my sister, "leave it or else I will beat you up." Food scrambles and fights were order of the day in the family I was raised. The size of one's meal would be determined by one's age. You had to fight for food at times, or else hunger would eat you alive. Living with ten siblings in a polygamous family is not the definition of tranquility. However, I have learned more from this revolving door than I could have been taught in solitary silence. Beyond chaos, there is a whisper that teaches the benefits of unselfish concern.

My mother was a teacher, but her salary could not sustain the big family. Almost every day, she would wake up early in the morning before work and go to the fields. My parents were shadowy figures whose voices I heard vaguely in the morning when sleep was shallow, and whom I glimpsed with irresistibly heavy eyelids as they trudged wearily into the house at night. We sat together as a whole family on special occasions. After a bumper harvest, my parents would sell their crops in the neighborhood. I vividly remember my mother counting proceeds from the crop sale, her dark face grim, and I think now, beautiful. Not with the hollow beauty of well-simulated features, but with a strong radiance of one who has suffered and never yielded. "This is for your school fees arrears," she would murmur, making a little pile. "This is for the groceries that we borrowed from Mr. Kibe's store," and so on. The list was endless. We would survive at least for the present.

My father instilled in me the importance of education. I would see the value of education every time I shook hands with him; the scratches and calluses from the field in his hands were enough motivation. After every award I received, he would firmly shake my hands as a sign of profound pride. My tacit prayer was to ease his pain one day. Unfortunately, this was never to come true, he died on 5 February 2016 in a car accident, only a week before I received my IGCSE O LEVEL results and I had attained 14 straight A grades, standing out to be one of the top performers in the country. After my father's death, his brothers took everything that he had acquired.

Inevitably, circumstances forced me to take a break from school in January 2017 and bear my share of the eternal burden at home. I had to take care of my mother whose health was deteriorating. I would spend the day doing household chores, and the nights were times of intensive study. It was on my mother's death-bed when I was fully convinced that she was a seasoned fighter. "Bradley," she called me, "I am not going to die till you finish school." In order not to disillusion that extraordinary faith in her voice, I assured her that she was going to live. Unfortunately, she succumbed to death on the 15th of March 2017. I "died" with her.

My belief in the God she had ardently prayed to till the time of her demise was shaken.

Already laid waste by poverty and pain, I went back to school through the generosity of strangers. School became a battleground for victory. I came back to life more determined than ever before. I out-performed the country boys who mocked my struggle. I went on to win accolades in the National and Regional Mathematics Olympiads and was awarded the Higher Life Foundation Scholarship that was going to pay my fees throughout high school.

Today, I am an epitome of a black, double-orphaned, African boy who lost everything he ever valued, but refused to give up on his dream.

REVIEW

What did the essay do well?

Bradley's essay begins with an anecdote of the usual morning scene in his kitchen. The clearly adversarial nature of his siblings' interactions over a plate of porridge certainly piques the reader's attention. Bradley then zooms out and discusses the values that growing up in a large family and experiencing the loss of his two parents taught him. Notice the emotional impact behind his words when he uses descriptive imagery and when readers are forced to grapple with lines such as "We would survive at least for the present."

Overall, Bradley highlights his diligence, tenacity, and selflessness in the face of all the hurdles that have been thrown his way and still manages to excel in all his pursuits. This essay gives the Admissions Committee a behind the curtain glimpse into Bradley's personal upbringing and family history, which is not immediately apparent in other parts of the Common Application.

What could be improved about the essay?

This essay focuses a lot on the hardships Bradley has experienced. However, more space could be dedicated to discussing the process of overcoming such hardships and the values and lessons that he carries with him today. While there is no perfect essay, writing about challenging experiences can be a great opportunity to highlight your resilience, but too much of a focus on what is lost may overwhelm a reader's perception of who you are as a person and not allow them to get to know you for your strengths.

What made this essay memorable?

The emotional impact of the entire essay and the vulnerability demonstrated by sharing a topic as difficult as death and loss is best punctuated by Bradley's final sentence. Laid out explicitly, the reality of his hardship is hard-hitting and impactful, allowing readers to really sit with the feelings elicited from the essay at the end.

—Christina Li

Laura W.

Hometown: Walsrode, Germany
High School: Public school, 1500 students in graduating class
GPA: 4.0 out of 4.0
SAT/ACT: undisclosed
Extracurriculars and Awards: Foreign Aid Club, first tenor saxophone in a band, piano, language clubs, entrepreneurship competitions, diplomacy projects, 4th place in German Startup Award
Major: Economics

ESSAY

Bridges

The first bridge I ever built was made of paper and glue.

My 8th grade physics teacher tasked my class with building a bridge out of two pieces of paper. Instead of focusing on the paper, I applied layers and layers of glue, strengthening the paper each time. The following week, the bridge successfully held 22 pounds, setting the highest school record in 12 years.

Two years later, I began building bridges of a different kind.

The car that brought me from the airport drove away, and I stepped through the doorway into the tiny apartment in the small city of Troyan, Bulgaria. The walls were covered with my stick-figure paintings and childhood pictures.

I laid my eyes on the wise woman in front of me and leaned down to pull her into a hug—not so tightly that it would break her, but enough to show my love. Raising her wrinkly hands to wipe my tears of joy away, my grandmother mumbled a row of Bulgarian words of affection and smiled. I didn't understand, but I smiled back.

Since she lives 1247.092 miles away from me, my grandmother is not always there to give me a hug when I need it most. Nevertheless, her heart of gold transcends physical distance and has taught me more than anyone about kindness, empathy, and compassion for others. Although she can't walk me through the intricacies of Bayesian statistics or neuroscience for my upcoming test, she tries her best to understand my ambitions and goals, and contributes in other ways—whenever I have an important test coming up, she prays, lights up candles, and keeps them lit until I'm done.

I could purchase plane tickets to trek the distance that separated our homes, but two other gaps were harder to traverse: my aging grandmother's health was deteriorating and I didn't speak Bulgarian.

I sought to create bridges to close these gaps.

My grandmother suffers from rheumatoid arthritis, a disease that presses her body from every side, deforming her joints, and arching her back. She is the smallest person I know, but yet for me, the greatest.

I wished that I could show her the world and take all her pain away, but the only thing that I could do for her was building a bridge that would connect her to the knowledge she wouldn't be able to access otherwise. I spent countless hours researching healthy meals to create a detoxifying and anti-inflammatory nutrition plan for her that would be easy to cook. The research paid off—the pain in her joints subsided.

When my grandmother and I "talked," emotions flowed between our souls like stars fly through space. Words would only describe what we feel—but not show. It was like listening to a song, but not paying attention to the lyrics, only to the pain and passion in the singer's voice and the flow of the melody.

In 2017, I decided that I finally wanted to learn Bulgarian. With a flashlight under my blanket, I started learning the Cyrillic alphabet, and Audio CD's with Bulgarian day-to-day conversations talked me to sleep. I surprised my grandmother by writing her a letter—written without Google Translate for the first time. Phone calls became much more frequent, and we grew closer together, but I wanted to go one step further. I moved to Bulgaria for a semester the year after in order to see her happy face when we could finally sing the song of our conversations—with the lyrics.

Seeing the influence my bridges had on my grandmother inspired me to build more. After I came back to Germany, I learned that bridges could be built between anyone.

In March 2020, my best friend's mother confided in me that she was overwhelmed with the task of coordinating her children's schoolwork at home during quarantine. It occurred to me that a platform for building bridges from younger students to older ones could take the load off of parents during this time. I quickly found that bridging these two groups of students leads to a higher learning efficiency since younger students often feel more comfortable studying with students that they can identify with. Soon, my startup was connecting a high-quality and often entirely subsidized learning resource to a socioeconomically diverse population of students from all over Germany.

I hope that by building bridges, we learn to better appreciate each other's differences in order to create a more empathetic and connected world—together.

My bridge made of paper and glue eventually collapsed after holding 22 pounds. But my next bridge is always stronger than the one before. Above all, I will continue connecting others, and I am excited to see what bridge I will build next.

REVIEW

What did the essay do well?

Laura chooses a simple but central theme to frame her essay: bridges. First, she shows her ingenuity with the literal bridge she opens her essay with, demonstrating a unique and interesting skill that reveals a bit about her interests and resourcefulness. Then she considers more metaphorical meanings of "bridge" and shows her dedication to the familial ties she builds with her grandma, demonstrating her ability to connect with others. Finally, she ties what the reader learned about her in the previous two sections and demonstrates her ingenuity by introducing her start-up at the end of the essay.

Moreover, throughout the essay Laura keeps her stories accessible—that is, she keeps things descriptive so we can walk with her through these memories and she doesn't use complicated vocabulary. This essay reads like a real person would talk, which is one of its strong points.

What could be improved about the essay?

The final section on Laura's start-up feels rushed because it condenses an entire accomplishment into one paragraph. Word count restrictions probably kicked in here, because we jump quickly from the problem to a potential solution to a high-level assessment of the program, which she only explains is a start-up at the end. Some more transitions in this section, or one or two more sentences to flesh out her start-up, would make this final bridge easier to understand.

What made this essay memorable?

It's refreshing to see a clearly structured and themed essay that strays away from clichés. Laura does not fall into the trap of overcomplicating her essay with superfluous words, and her voice is very clear. This makes readers find it unique among a sea of essays that likely read as disingenuous.

—Cara Chang

V.
PASSIONS

Sarika C.

Hometown: Acton, Massachusetts, USA
High School: Public school, 500 students in graduating class
GPA: 3.966 out of 4.0 (4.702 Weighted)
SAT: 1580
Extracurriculars and Awards: Summer research intern in MIT biology lab, editor-in-chief of school literary magazine, co-founder and co-president of school Girls in Science Club, co-leader of school Indian-fusion a cappella group, tutor in school writing center, member of school choruses, mentor for Coursera courses, TEDx speaker on perceptions of disability, regional Scholastic Art & Writing Awards winner, National Merit Semifinalist, National Honor Society member, Wellesley College Book Award recipient, MA Foreign Language Association essay contest honorable mention winner
Major: Computer Science

ESSAY

I, Too, Can Dance

I was in love with the way the dainty pink mouse glided across the stage, her tutu twirling as she pirouetted and her rose-colored bow following the motion of her outstretched arms with every grand jeté.

I had always dreamed I would dance, and Angelina Ballerina made it seem so easy. There was something so freeing about the way she wove her body into the delicate threads of the Sugar Plum Fairy's song each time she performed an arabesque. I longed for my whole being to melt into the magical melodies of music; I longed to enchant the world with my own stories; and I longed for the smile that glimmered on every dancer's face.

At recess, my friends and I would improvise dances. But while they seemed well on their way to achieving ballerina status, my figure eights were more like zeroes and every attempt at spinning around left me feeling dizzy. Sometimes, I even ran over my friends' toes. How could I share my stories with others if I managed to injure them with my wheelchair before the story even began?

I then tried piano, but my fingers stumbled across the keys in an uncoordinated staccato tap dance of sorts. I tried art, but the clumsiness of my brush left the canvas a colorful mess. I tried the recorder, but had Angelina existed in real life, my rendition of "Mary Had a Little Lamb" would have frozen her in midair, with flute-like screeches tumbling through the air, before ending in an awkward split and shattering the gossamer world the Sugar Plum Fairy had worked so hard to build.

For as long as I could remember, I'd also been fascinated by words, but I'd never explored writing until one day in fourth grade, the school librarian announced a poetry contest. That night, as I tried to sleep, ideas scampered through my head like Nutcracker mice awakening a sleeping Clara to a mystical new world. By morning, I had choreographed the mice to tell a winning story in verse about all the marvelous outer space factoids I knew.

Now, my pencil pirouettes perfect O's on paper amidst sagas of doting mothers and evanescent lovers. The tip of my pen stipples the lines of my notebook with the tale of a father's grief, like a ballerina tiptoeing en pointe; as the man finds solace in nature, the ink flows gracefully, and for a moment, it leaps off the page, as if reaching out to the heavens to embrace his daughter's soul. Late at night, my fingers tap dance across the keys of my laptop, tap tap tapping an article about the latest breakthrough in cancer research—maybe LDCT scans or aneuploidy-targeted therapy could have saved the daughter's life; a Spanish poem about the beauty of unspoken moments; and the story of a girl in a wheelchair who learned how to dance.

As the world sleeps, I lose myself in the cathartic cadences of fresh ink, bursting with stories to be told and melting into parched paper. I cobble together phrases until they spring off my tongue, as if the Sugar Plum Fairy herself has transformed the staccato rumblings of my brain into something legato and sweet. I weave my heart, my soul, my very being into my words as I read them out loud, until they become almost like a chant. With every rehearsal, I search for the perfect finale to complete my creation. When I finally find it, eyes dry with midnight-induced euphoria, I remember that night so many years ago when I discovered the magic of writing, and smile.

I may not dance across the stage like Angelina Ballerina, but I can dance across the page.

I, too, can dance.

REVIEW
What did the essay do well?

The author's whimsical language engages the reader throughout, using the connecting thread of Angelina Ballerina to speak about her variety of interests, passions, and talents. The writing style itself is very creative and fun, tying ballet terms to the motions of writing, playing instruments, and more. This whimsy and thematic description is consistent throughout the essay, establishing a strong and compelling authorial voice.

In terms of the content of the essay, touching on both successes and failures humanizes Sarika without spending too much time focusing on those weaknesses. Instead, it is endearing to see her experiment with other interests like art and music, which are ultimately a part of her path to finding her real passion in writing. This essay is also strong in that by the nature of its medium, she is able to exhibit the very writing skills that are the focus of the essay.

What could be improved about the essay?

This essay includes a title that is also repeated as the final line of the piece. While in this case the title establishes the theme of dance and intentionally misdirects the reader to make the actual ending more surprising, it is not entirely necessary. Titles can sometimes be a divisive topic when it comes to personal statements and including one can be a personal choice, but overall most essays stand stronger without a title but with an interesting hook.

What made this essay memorable?

The unique theme of this essay along with the whimsical language and creativity in writing makes it stick out from other, less narrative essays that most students produce. Additionally, the author's inclusion of sentimental moments as a child adds an emotional component to the essay.

—Isabella Tran

Daniella Z.

Hometown: Newton, Massachusetts, USA
High School: Public school, 450 students in graduating class
GPA: 4.0 out of 4.0 (5.0 Weighted)
SAT: 1540
Extracurriculars and Awards: Editor-in-chief of school newspaper (several national and regional distinctions), classical piano and chamber music (New England regional awards), involved in Jewish youth groups, worked in doctor's office over the summer, chemistry olympiad school representative
Major: Applied Math

ESSAY

Each time I bake cookies, they come out differently. Butter, sugar, eggs, flour—I measure with precision, stir with vigor, then set the oven to 375°F. The recipe is routine, yet hardly redundant.

After a blizzard left me stranded indoors with nothing but a whisk and a pantry full of the fundamentals, I made my first batch: a tray of piping hot chocolate chunkers whose melt-in-the-mouth morsels comforted my snowed-in soul. Such a flawless description, however, belies my messy process. In reality, my method was haphazard and carefree, the cookies a delicious fortuity that has since been impossible to replicate.

Each subsequent batch I make is a gamble. Will the cookies flatten and come out crispy? Stay bulbous and gooey? Am I a bad baker, or are they inherently capricious? Even with a recipe book full of suggestions, I can never place a finger on my mistake. The cookies are fickle and short-tempered. Baking them is like walking on egg-shells—and I have an empty egg carton to prove it. Perhaps beginner's luck had been the secret ingredient all along.

Yet, curiosity keeps me flipping to the same page in my recipe book. I became engrossed in perfecting the cookies not by the mechanical satisfaction of watching ingredients combine into batter, but by the chance to wonder at simplicity. The inconsistency is captivating. It is, after all, a strict recipe, identical ingredients combined in the same permutation. How can such orthodox steps yield such radical, unpredictable results? Even with the most formulaic tasks, I am questioning the universe.

Chemistry explains some of the anomaly. For instance, just a half-pinch extra of baking soda can have astounding ramifications on how the dough bubbles. The kitchen became my laboratory: I diaried each trial like a scientist; I bought a scale for more accurate measurements; I borrowed "On Food and Cooking: The Science and Lore of the Kitchen" from the library. But all to no avail—the variables refused to come together in any sort of equilibrium.

I then approached the problem like a pianist, taking the advice my teacher wrote in the margins of my sheet music and pouring it into the mixing bowl. There are 88 pitches on a keyboard, and there are a dozen ingredients in the recipe. To create a rhapsodic dessert, I needed to understand all of the melodic and harmonic lines and how they complemented one another. I imagined the recipe in Italian script, the chocolate chips as quick staccatos suspended in a thick adagio medium. But my fingers always stumbled at the coda of each performance, the details of the cookies turning to a hodgepodge of sound.

I whisk, I sift, I stir, I pre-heat the oven again, but each batch has its flaws, either too sweet, burnt edges, grainy, or underdone.

Though the cookies were born of boredom, their erratic nature continues to fascinate me. Each time my efforts yield an imperfect result, I develop resilience to return the following week with a fresh apron, ready to try again. I am mesmerized by the quirks of each trial. It isn't enough to just mix and eat—I must understand.

My creative outlook has kept the task engaging. Despite the repetition in my process, I find new angles that liven the recipe. In college and beyond, there will be things like baking cookies, endeavors that seem so unvaried they risk spoiling themselves to a housewife's drudgery. But from my time in the kitchen, I have learned how to probe deeper into the mechanics of my tasks, to bring music into monotony, and to turn work into play. However the cookie crumbles in my future, I will approach my work with curiosity, creativity, and earnestness.

REVIEW

What did the essay do well?

Daniella's detailed writing using imagery and technical flair brings life to her essay. The varied appearance, taste, and textures of all her cookie experiments strongly come across and the essay itself mimics the author's process of baking with its repetition and new angles. This appeal to the senses along with the narrative voice and variety in sentence lengths work to make the essay particularly engaging. The personification of the cookies also showcases the author's writing abilities and her creativity beyond the example.

This essay is also strong in that it seamlessly moves from the primary topic of baking to engage with Daniella's other interests in chemistry and piano.

What could be improved about the essay?

While a lot of the writing is strong, some stylistic choices felt extraneous. For example, the use of semicolons in paragraph 5 and some word choices prevent the essay from feeling entirely genuine. The other place for improvement here is in conveying the final overall message of the essay, which is slightly unclear as it stands. The reader is left wondering beyond Daniella's interests whether the experiences described in her essay should inform them of her approach to learning, her personality, or her goals.

What made this essay memorable?

What is most memorable about this essay to me was the almost poetic or rhythmic quality to the writing as Daniella weaves between her topics. Overall, the author's ability to take a mundane task such as baking and creatively turn it into a captivating essay while tying in her experiences with chemistry and piano enables this essay to stand out against those of other applicants. Additionally, the author's interesting hook captures the reader, as "each time I bake cookies, they come out differently" seems basic at first but draws in the reader to understand why.

—Isabella Tran

SAMANTHA C.

Hometown: Los Angeles, California, USA
High School: Private school, 86 students in graduating class
GPA: 4.51 out of 4.0
ACT: 36
Extracurriculars and Awards: Violin, figure skating, independent social science research, school newspaper, school literary magazine, international literary magazine, community service (creative writing program for students), National Merit Commended Scholar, Cum Laude Society, Scholastic Art and Writing Awards (x6), USFSA Graduating Senior (Gold Level), California Scholarship Federation
Major: English

ESSAY

I've always been a storyteller, but I've only been an alleged fish killer since age five. As a child, my head was so filled up with stories that I might have forgotten to feed Bubbles the class pet just one time too often. Once I pulverized an entire pencil, because I was daydreaming instead of taking it out of the sharpener.

More than anything else, I became an obsessive list-maker. I memorized and wrote down long lists of my stuffed animals, cities around the world, and my favorite historical time periods. I created itineraries and packing lists for my Build-A-Bears, then arranged them in rows on a pretend airplane. I drew family trees for a made-up family during the Industrial Revolution. I wrote lists until the spine of my notebook cracked under the weight of graphite.

For a long time, I thought this was something that I alone did, and that I did alone. Lying on the floor of my bedroom, I spun fantastical stories of mundane events. Each story opened and closed in my head, untold and unsung.

Years later, though—to my amazement—I discovered other people who were interested in the same things I was. Wandering into fanfiction websites and online forums, I was welcomed into a vibrant community of writers—serious, silly, passionate people who wrote hundreds of thousands of words analyzing character dynamics and exploring endless plot threads. When I finally started posting my own thoughts, I didn't feel like I was taking a risk or venturing into new territory. I had been speaking these words to myself since I was five, preparing myself to finally shout them into the real world. And people responded.

Spurred on by this excitement, I started writing stories for other people to read. I had fallen in love with the community writing had given me, and with writing itself. I wanted to contribute my own small piece to a world much bigger than me. I shouted my stories up to the Wi-Fi signals that caught and carried them, waiting to be found by someone else writing lists in her bedroom alone.

In high school, I also found joy in editing. I loved analyzing, polishing, and curating my classmates' short stories, poems, and artwork to make them shine for my school's literary magazine. I spent hours with other editors, passionately arguing the merits and weaknesses of dozens of writing pieces. Editing the school newspaper, meanwhile, became a way to spotlight members of the school community, from profiling new staff and faculty to polling the student body about the stigma surrounding menstruation.

I've now had my poems published in a national literary journal and have joined the editorial staff of an international literary magazine for teens. I feel like I'm discovering my power, and with it my ability to create change. Last year, I founded SPEAK, a creative writing program for elementary school students. I wanted to assist younger writers so they could create their own communities. During SPEAK sessions, I taught a group of students how to draw a map of a fantasy wolf kingdom they had designed, helped a girl edit her classmate's poem about hulahoops, and listened to a third-grader talk faster and faster as we discussed the meaning of soup in *The Tale of Despereaux*.

I've now turned SPEAK into a self-sustaining club at my school, and I'm expanding the program onto an online platform. Writing changed my life, but it only happened when I started sharing my work, putting it out there, and starting conversations—not just responding. Alone, stories used to abstract me from the outside world. Now, stories connect me to the world, creating communities instead of pulling me away from them. For too many of us, our stories are born in our heads, and they die there. I'm going to change that, for myself and for as many people as I can bring with me.

REVIEW

What did the essay do well?

Samantha does a great job of taking the reader through all the ways she loves writing and all the while giving readers an impression of her caring and passionate nature. She starts with her writing—what it means to her and her identity—and then moves on to editing and SPEAK, which shows her compassion and proves that there is weight to her conviction that "writing changed my life."

One of the great strengths of this essay is that Samantha keeps a human, even casual tone. At no point does the reader feel like she is exaggerating or flaunting accomplishments—her language is simple yet descriptive. When one chooses to highlight writing as a skill in the essay, the stakes are raised considerably higher to illustrate that talent more so than any other since the essay is itself a reflection of that skill. By writing concisely, Samantha demonstrates her strengths without relying on flourishes or embellishments to support her essay.

What could be improved about the essay?

The hook (very first paragraph), while striking, didn't connect smoothly into the rest of the essay, especially relative to the other transitions, such as the one between the second and third paragraph. Calling herself "an alleged fish killer" is funny, as is the image that she "pulverized an entire pencil," but it's unclear how that relates to writing. The second paragraph could have served as a stronger introduction.

What made this essay memorable?

In 649 words, Samantha not only takes us through her journey as a writer, managing to touch on several aspects of her passion, but also points to the future with a meaningful conclusion that shows her character: "For too many of us, our stories are born in our heads, and they die there. I'm going to change that, for myself and for as many people as I can bring with me."

—Cara Chang

Georgina Y.

Hometown: Brockton, Massachusetts, USA
High School: Public school, 989 students in graduating class
GPA: 4.0 out of 4.0 (4.969 Weighted)
SAT/ACT: undisclosed
Extracurriculars and Awards: Co-founder and president of
Model Brockton City Council, captain at Denise Buote Dance
Studio, student representative for Brockton School Com-
mittee, class secretary for Junior and Senior Executive Com-
mittee, advanced concert band, wind ensemble, marching
band, president of St. Theresa Maronite Youth Organization,
president of Foreign Language Honor Society, clerk/elections
inspector at City of Brockton Elections Commission, social media manager at Nail Bar & Spa, Brockton High School Halftime
Majorettes, Seal of Biliteracy in Mandarin Chinese, Harvard's
Undergraduate Women in Business Ambassador, Harvard's
Summer Business Academy, Superintendent's Award, 1st place
at Bryant's Global Leadership Summer Program G-Pitch Business Presentation
Major: Economics

ESSAY
When Life Doesn't Give You Lemons . . .

With the blazing morning sun beaming through the window, I had
an inclination to make a stand to sell Lebanese laymounada—a
light lemonade flavored with a splash of rosewater. Throughout my
childhood, anytime the temperature spiked over seventy degrees,

there would be laymounada waiting for me at my Teta's (grand-mother in Lebanese Arabic) house.

At that moment, I scoured the cabinets and secured the glass pitcher only to realize we did not have lemons. To my disappoint-ment, I realized my days of being an entrepreneur and generating revenue from my laymounada stand were over before they could even begin. I sat at the kitchen table, wallowing in disappointment. I wanted everyone to be able to taste my Teta's laymounada. Sud-denly, I had an idea that would either prove to be inventive or a total failure. I would sell lemonade without the lemons. Revolution-ary, right?

I ripped off a rectangular sheet of paper towel and jotted down my business plan. I listed the key elements of the business plan: a drawing of a cup, a rose, and the price—"fifty scents"—to corre-late with the rose-themed business. I sat outside of my childhood home located in a cul-de-sac of five houses and sold my neighbors a rose drink—a combination of filtered water, packets of sugar, and a dash of rosewater. Granted, I only made about $10 from a com-bination of my parents and generous neighbors who did not drink the "lemonade," but the experience allowed me to realize regard-less of the obstacle, if you are passionate, you can persevere. Teta's laymounada was my introduction to entrepreneurship.

The entrepreneurial skills gained from my laymounada stand allowed me to establish A&G Jewelry, co-founded with my sister when I was twelve. This business focused on representing our Leba-nese heritage. Using supplies we found around our house and from our local craft store, we created a variety of pieces that featured tra-ditional Middle Eastern coins, beads, and clay baked into the shape of Lebanon. My sister and I collaborated to create marketing tools to promote our new business. Before we knew it, A&G Jewelry had

earned a spot at my church's annual Lebanese festival. After tirelessly marketing and selling our jewelry for three days straight, we
had made over $900 in revenue, which we decided to donate to the
church.

Entrepreneurship took a new form in high school when my sister
and I founded our second partnership, The Model Brockton City
Council. We saw a need to engage our peers in local government
by designing a simulation of our city council. We had to collect sig-
natures, present to many administrators, and market our new club.
The initial goal to have more people try my lemonade resonated
with me as I strived to have more people engage in their civic duties. Today, over twenty-five of my classmates frequently attend my
meetings.

With my first business venture selling laymounada, I made $10;
with A&G Jewelry, $900; with the Model Brockton City Council,
the revenue amounted to $0. Although there was not a financial
gain, I attained experience as a negotiator, problem solver, creative
thinker, and most importantly, I became persistent.

Twelve years have passed since that summer day with my "laymounada," and I have yet to maintain a long-lasting business. My
six-year-old self would have seen this lack of continuity as a co-
lossal failure, but instead, it instilled an intense curiosity in me.
Little did I know the experience would remain so vivid after all
these years. It has continued to push me, compelling me to challenge myself both academically and entrepreneurially. As I grow
older, my intrinsic drive to have a lemonade stand, regardless of
whatever obstacles come my way, persists as a deep-seated love of
business.

When life doesn't give you lemons, still make lemonade (or laymounada, as my Teta would say).

REVIEW

What did the essay do well?

Georgina takes a core childhood memory and develops it into a narrative of entrepreneurship that is fundamentally grounded in interacting with and impacting the communities she belongs to, from her neighbors to her church to the entire city. Beyond this, she includes just the right level of descriptive detail to immerse the reader in specific scenes and experiences like her makeshift rosewater recipe or her model city council tasks, while still prioritizing the overall arc of the narrative. The language is also clear and cogent, with smooth transitions between different memories and time periods in her life. Lastly, the essay's clear structural organization renders it very easy for the reader to follow, allowing the ending to wrap everything up in a well-anticipated final point that mirrors the title.

What could be improved about the essay?

The concrete metrics provided throughout Georgina's essay actually detract slightly from her ultimate point: that entrepreneurship does not necessarily need to be measured by revenue, but by the skills it fosters. However, after she makes this point early on through the rosewater stand, the emphasis on the material success of her jewelry business conflicts with both the first memory and the subsequent admission that the city council initiative also did not result in revenue. A stronger sense of future direction and ambition beyond simply being "persistent" would have been beneficial.

What made this essay memorable?

The inversion of a static, well-known metaphor (when life gives you lemons . . .) and specific cultural references to language create an authentic voice. This allows readers to easily attach their own experiences to the hook of the essay since Georgina gives it a tagline of sorts. Additionally, the author's use of vivid action to showcase her personal traits instead of simply stating them better reveals to the reader that she is a self-starter.

—Cynthia Lu

Rosanna K.

Hometown: Helsinki, Finland
High School: Public school, 150 students in graduating class
GPA: 8.5 out of 10
SAT/ACT: undisclosed
Extracurriculars and Awards: Student body secretary, valedictorian
Major: Economics

ESSAY

"Fashion on Wheels, a clothing brand for wheelchair users." I was standing in front of the classroom, the first student of the group to present our business ideas at a facultative entrepreneurship course. I noticed the perplexed looks of my classmates. This was something unexpected.

I have spent my life learning to communicate with my brother Roni, who speaks mostly through reciting cartoon lines. I am used to scrutinizing each label at the supermarket so that our groceries contain no traces of nuts, and thoroughly planning my activities so that Roni is not home alone for more than fourteen seconds.

When I was younger, my life situation often irritated me. I fantasized about family vacations to Italy and getting help with homework. Instead, I had Sunday walks to our local train station so that Roni could marvel at the passing trains, and my study sessions were disturbed by him coming to my room. Apparently, my 107 square foot room is the best place to mirror himself and showcase his musical talent by drumming on an empty yogurt can and humming his own obscure 6-minute composition.

As the vice president of the Roni club, my duties include taking him to the dentist and for walks, gaining looks from passersby as I firmly grab his hand to prevent him from running into a trench every time he sees a dog nearby. I need to take the lead when he decides to lie on the floor in the middle of a crowded mall. Gradually, I have responded to the ogles with a smile and learned to handle him in different settings so that he can experience as much as his limitations allow. Nowadays I can confidently take him even to the quiet museums and proudly wear matching Mickey Mouse T-Shirts.

At home, I am also the head of the peacekeeping department. In our big, eclectic family, occasional conflicts are inevitable. Whenever those disputes overheat Roni, he storms into my room, his safe haven. I always let him stay with me and rage his anxiety away, even when I am studying for the most crucial exams or reading the most thrilling philosophy articles on phenomenology. Weathering these moments has taught me uttermost patience and resilience.

Besides, Roni has helped me discover the significance of seemingly mundane things. I admire his genuine love for something so "dull" as public transportation. His room walls are lined with his drawings of Helsinki metro route maps, he carries his EpiPen in a blue tram-printed bag, and nothing in the world makes his eyes sparkle like going for a bus ride. If he was invited to meet the president, the only thing he would care about is how we travel there.

I wish my brother could know how drastically he has shaped my life. Befriending my wheelchaired and hearing-impaired Shed-Helsinki peers and being equal on stage with them, I learned more than I probably would have from a leading role in the National Theatre. Without my brother's influence, the chance would have passed me by.

With his special needs come special abilities: he can see details most are blind to. That has inspired me. Fashion on Wheels was only a minor piece of homework, but I treated it as if I was a Nobel prize nominee presenting my breakthrough research paper. With the project, I was able to convey the values formed by my distinct experiences to the world I value the most: academia.

At the end of the class, we voted for the best business idea. When I was announced the winner, my face lit up as if I had just become Prime Minister. My external reward was an ice cream cone from the school cafeteria paid for by the teacher, but I considered the project an immense internal victory. I had used my background to inspire others. At that moment, I knew that is what I want to continue doing.

Sitting around the schoolyard after the class, I watched my friend indulging in the victory ice cream I gave her and thought how wonderful my offbeat family is.

REVIEW

What did the essay do well?

This essay portrayed Rosanna's personal struggles, interests, and life through subtle storytelling. It begins by throwing the reader into a familiar setting—giving a presentation in class. Rather than simply telling the reader her situation as a high-achieving student as well as sister to a brother with special needs, she uses a collection of anecdotes to portray her life as she sees it. The reader can't help but empathize with Rosanna, admire her passionate approach to all aspects of her life, and appreciate the honesty with which she approached this essay. In the end, she comes full circle by returning to the high school setting, concluding the story after giving the appropriate background, and she even sprinkles in some fun details to further elaborate on her character.

Overall, Rosanna guides the reader to draw the conclusions she wants them to draw by illustrating her growth as a sister and as a person; one can't help but want her to succeed.

What could be improved about the essay?

Rosanna's descriptive language is excellent throughout the essay, and while much of the description of her brother ties into her role as a caregiver and sister, there are a few moments in the essay that are exclusively about her brother, such as the sixth paragraph; she only says she admires his appreciation for public transport instead of tying in how her brother's love for the mundane has shaped her.

What made this essay memorable?

Her attention to detail and descriptive language: "my 107 square foot room," "as the vice president of the Roni club," "external reward" and "internal victory," and many more creative uses of language were all vehicles for effectively communicating a life story filled with challenge in an enjoyable and easy-to-read fashion.

—Liam Peterson

Clara N.

Hometown: Boynton Beach, Florida, USA
High School: Private school, 200 students in graduating class
GPA: 5.22 out of 4.33
SAT: 1580
Extracurriculars and Awards: Classical piano, C2-level fluency in French, German, Italian, and Spanish, valedictorian, National AP Scholar, NCTE Certificate of Superior Writing
Major: Economics

ESSAY

My nightstand is home to a small menagerie of critters, each glass-eyed specimen lovingly stuffed with cotton. Don't get the wrong idea, now—I'm not a taxidermist or anything. I crochet.

Crochet is a family tradition. My grandmother used to wield her menacing steel hook like a mage's staff and tout it as such: an instrument that bestowed patience, decorum, and poise on its owner. During her youth in Vietnam, she spent her evenings designing patterns for ornate doilies and handkerchiefs. Then the Vietnam War turned our family into refugees. The Viet Cong imprisoned my grandfather, a colonel in the South Vietnam Air Force, in a grueling labor camp for thirteen years. Many wives would have lost hope, but my grandmother was no average woman. A literature professor in a time when women's access to education was limited, she assumed the role of matriarch with wisdom and confidence, providing financial and emotional security. As luxuries like yarn grew scarce, she conjured up all sorts of useful household items—durable pillowcases, blankets, and winter coats—and taught my mother to do the same. Because of these bitter wartime memories, she wanted my handiwork to be of a decidedly less practical bent; among the first objects she taught me to crochet were chrysanthemums and roses. However, making flowers bloom from yarn was no easy task.

Even with its soft plastic grip and friendly rounded edges, my first crochet hook had a mind of its own, like the enchanted broom in "The Sorcerer's Apprentice." It stubbornly disobeyed my orders as I impatiently wrenched it through the yarn. My grandmother's stern appraisal of my efforts often interrupted this perpetual tug-of-war: My stitches were uneven. The edges curled inward. I would unravel my work and start anew.

I convinced myself that cobbling together a lopsided rectangle would be the pinnacle of my crochet prowess but refused to give up. Just as a diligent wizard casts more advanced spells over time, I learned to channel the magic of the crochet hook. The animal kingdom is my main source of inspiration; the diversity and vivid pigmentation of life on Earth lend themselves perfectly to the vibrant and versatile art of crochet. Many of the animals I make embark on migratory journeys, like their real-life counterparts. Take Agnes, for example, a cornflower-blue elephant named after mathematician Maria Gaetana Agnesi who lives in my calculus teacher's classroom, happily grazing on old pencil shavings and worksheets. As I fasten off the final stitches on every creature, I hope to weave a little whimsy and color into someone's life.

Each piece I finish reminds me of the network of stitches that connects mother and daughter, past and present, tradition and innovation. In this vast cultural web, I am proud to be my family's link between East and West. As I prepare for adulthood, I am eager to weave my own mark into the great patchwork quilt that is America.

REVIEW

What did the essay do well?

Clara's essay begins with a hook, explaining her collection of stuffed and "glass-eyed" creatures, but the first paragraph is short and punchy, asserting the narrative voice and flair. She then pivots to explaining her background in crochet, having learned from her grandmother, and how her grandmother used crocheting to adapt and survive when her family became refugees from the war.

The harsh realities of the author's grandmother's experiences are juxtaposed with the magical and imaginative qualities of Clara's crocheting, but both mirror a journey of resilience and growth. Finally, by connecting her hobby to a larger part of her identity, she communicates her interest and devotion to history, family, and learning. Overall, this essay is thoughtfully written to convey Clara's nonacademic hobbies and interests, as well as her character and what is important to her—things that are not showcased in any other aspect of the Common Application.

What could be improved about the essay?

The second-to-last paragraph where Clara talks about improving in crochet could do more to explain how and why she was able to improve aside from just not giving up. It also could connect more clearly to her overall themes in the essay as it does not contribute as much as the other paragraphs and feels somewhat off topic when switching gears from exploring her familial history to narrating about the animal kingdom.

What made this essay memorable?

Clara's unusual hobby of crochet is a great device to set up a personable and shining story of familial memory, experience, and connection, making Clara stand out and bringing her to life for readers. Additionally, her use of real-world examples, such as Agnes, adds a personal emotional touch to the essay.

—Isabella Tran

BILLY B.

Hometown: Salem, Massachusetts, USA
High School: Public school, 200 students in graduating class
GPA: 4.77 out of 5.0 (Weighted)
SAT: 1560
Extracurriculars and Awards: Class vice president, Student Council co-president, National Honor Society, National Green School Society, Harvard Book Award, captain of varsity cross country, swimming, and track and field teams
Major: Engineering Sciences on the Environmental Engineering Track

ESSAY

As I rode up and down the gentle slopes of the Peabody skatepark, I watched my younger brother race down from the highest point on the halfpipe and fly past me at the speed of light. I wish I could do that, I thought, eyeing the enormous curve that towered over me. But I didn't dare make my way up to the top. Instead, I stuck with the routine I was comfortable with, avoiding the steep inclines at all costs.

Each week during the summer before my fourth-grade year, my brother and I would visit that same skatepark, and I would take my mini BMX bike to the bottom of that monstrous ramp, ready to attack the giant. I started off low reaching only a quarter of the way up at first, too scared to go any higher. But each week, I gained more confidence and kept reaching greater heights. Halfway there, two-thirds, three-quarters. Until finally, I mustered up enough courage to complete my final challenge.

With my brother's shouts of joy ringing in my ears, it seemed as though the concrete mass was calling my name, drawing me closer and closer, until I couldn't resist its pleading any further. I walked my bike up the stairs and approached the steep drop-off. My hands started to sweat and my legs began to shake as I inched toward the edge, staring in the face of doom. Finally at the lip of the ramp, I paused briefly, took a deep breath, and moved forward just enough to send myself speeding downwards. I couldn't contain my excitement as my "Woooo!" echoed around the park. I had finally ridden down the tallest ramp!

Throughout my life I have enjoyed having a plan and being in control. When working in a group, I make sure that everyone knows exactly which aspect of the project they will complete. I organize all my homework in a planner so that I never miss a due date. Each night, I outline my schedule for the following day so that I know what meetings, sports events, and other activities I have to attend. When I visited New York City over the summer, I prepared a detailed itinerary to follow. Rarely is there a day when I don't have a general idea of what I'm going to do, but sometimes my plan doesn't correlate with how the day truly plays out.

Over the years, I have learned to adapt when situations take an unexpected turn, and, similar to that time at the skatepark, I have been able to step out of my comfort zone more often. It isn't the end of the world when things don't go exactly as planned; oftentimes, sudden changes and new experiences make for a more enjoyable and interesting time. As much as I enjoy a strict itinerary, some of my best nights have begun by hopping in the car with my friends, picking a direction, and going wherever the wind takes us. As hard as I try to plan out my day, an unforeseen event is almost inevitable. Although this can bring about some stress, scrambling around to figure things out is not only an essential skill, but can be a fun challenge, too.

I can't imagine a completely organized life without a little uncertainty. Unexpected circumstances are bound to occur, and making the most of them is one of my favorite parts of life. Regardless of how much I love having a plan, my flexibility and willingness to step out of my comfort zone is something I have and will always take pride in.

REVIEW

What did the essay do well?

There is a well-organized structure, with an introduction, a body, and a conclusion. The author presents a clear theme of stepping out of comfort zones and adapting to unexpected circumstances. It also includes specific examples to illustrate the theme, such as the writer's experiences at the skatepark and in New York City. The essay includes personal details and anecdotes that make it more engaging and relatable for the reader, concluding with a statement about the writer's pride in his flexibility and willingness to step out of his comfort zone, which ties back to the theme of the essay and provides a sense of closure.

What could be improved about the essay?

The opening paragraph could be more engaging. Instead of starting with a general statement about the skatepark, the writer could try beginning with a specific, vivid detail that draws the reader in. The essay could also benefit from more development of the theme of stepping out of comfort zones. While Billy touches on this topic in the second half of the essay, it would be helpful to have more examples and elaboration on how the writer has learned to adapt and embrace unexpected circumstances. Finally, the essay could use more transitional phrases to connect the different parts and create a smoother flow. This could help the essay feel more cohesive and make it easier for the reader to follow the writer's thoughts.

What made this essay memorable?

The author is able to demonstrate his growth and the unpredictable nature of life in a humble yet engaging tone. Many applicants often come across arrogant and brash, unlike Billy's essay, which welcomes the reader into exploring his personal life without reservations.

—Calvin Beighle

Gracia P.

Hometown: Calumet, Michigan, USA
High School: Public school, 100 students in graduating class
GPA: 4.0 out of 4.0
SAT/ACT: undisclosed
Extracurriculars and Awards: Pep Club president, SADD chapter vice president, marching band, pep band, concert band, drumline, Junior R.O.T.C. (skating color guard, drill team, choir), National Honor Society, cheerleading, figure skating
Major: English

ESSAY

Xué wú zhìjìng.
(There is no limit in learning.)

For as long as I can remember, I have been fascinated by foreign languages. I've always tried to immerse myself in language, from listening to Spanish songs on the radio to intently concentrating on the waitress at the Chinese restaurant. There is just something about the complexities of language and words that compels me to dig deeper into understanding it.

Language to me is a beautiful puzzle; as I progress through learning and understanding, the pieces fall into place. It wasn't until the sixth grade that I decided to pursue this interest, up to this point it had simply been a subject to ponder. After watching a video on the Great Wall of China, an urge to look into the Chinese language overpowered me. The eloquence of the language was music to my ears, and although I did not know what was being said, a desire formed to find out. I took to the Internet, searching pages of textbooks and dictionaries. I visited the library and checked out books on language and culture.

A need to widen my knowledge grew inside of me and having the resources to do so at my fingertips was a luxury. Studying the Chinese language became a frequent occurrence in my free time. When I entered high school, my opportunities for learning expanded. Sophomore year I spoke to my counselor about taking a Chinese 1 course online and after some digging, he was able to enroll me in the class. I had never before been so excited to take a course. I diligently worked in my online classroom, I took notes and studied tirelessly for quizzes. I began to take my studies outside of school, I set my phone to display Chinese along with English and contacted the local college to get in touch with Chinese-speaking students.

The next year I took Chinese 2 and treasured every moment. This year I planned to take both Chinese 3 and 4, however, my school had no further enrollment options for advancement in the subject. I was originally disappointed, I had been ready to continue my journey into the Chinese language. I was not going to let this set back my passion for foreign language, and I am now happily enrolled in Spanish 1.

Learning Chinese blossomed into so much more than just a class, it allowed me the opportunity to learn about myself and progress my level of intelligence. I am grateful every day that I live in a generation in which I am able to plunge into a new language and culture. I feel that by surrounding myself with foreign language, I am developing a much greater world of opportunities and achievements. My foreign language journey does not end here—I plan to continue my education throughout college, my career, and the rest of my life. As long as the opportunity to learn exists, I intend to always take it.

REVIEW
What did the essay do well?

This essay starts with a good, engaging opening. Sometimes, titles, quotes or similar modes of opening are unnecessary for personal statement essays, but the choice to include the Chinese text suits Gracia's essay according to both its topic and its message. Her first paragraph to follow the opener is also particularly strong, using sensory details of "Spanish songs on the radio" to ground the author's passion for languages.

What could be improved about the essay?

One flaw in this essay is the vagueness behind some of the author's feelings and reasons for pursuing language. There are many abstract ideas that seem to direct her towards it, and exploring at least one concrete experience with greater description may better illustrate a compelling narrative. The language would also be a bit more polished if the author cut out things such as the unnecessary passive voice in this sentence in paragraph 3: "Studying the Chinese language became a frequent occurrence in my free time."

While it is sometimes good to remain very focused on a topic in the personal statement so as to not confuse the reader, there is also definitely room for expansion in this essay. The small details provided at the beginning of the author's interest in other languages are briefly touched upon near the end when the author mentions taking Spanish classes. But if the goal of the essay was to express interest in foreign languages more generally, these details could be woven more frequently throughout the essay.

What made this essay memorable?

The author's ability to showcase her strong passions and curiosity for language through a narrative tone allows her to express to the reader that she is an inquisitive, passionate, and dedicated student who would be an asset to the academic community at college.

—Isabella Tran

MAIA P.

Hometown: Arlington, Massachusetts, USA
High School: Public school, 330 students in graduating class
GPA: 3.69 out of 4.0 (4.45 Weighted)
SAT/ACT: undisclosed
Extracurriculars and Awards: Class vice president (4 years),
varsity soccer and track and field (4 years for both, soccer
captain senior year), co-founded Anti-Racism Working Group,
National Honor Society, tutoring, Relay for Life student coordi-
nator and event planner
Major: Social Studies

ESSAY

Push forward, pull back, pivot, again.

Beads of sweat rhythmically descended from my hairline to my
brow, then down my chin. The machine's steady drone shook the
handle, sending a vibration from my fingertips to my head, tick-
ling my ears. The freshly cut grass poked up between my toes, both
prickly and soft at the same time. Holding back a sneeze, my nose
tingled with the sharp smell of the half-cut grass blades trailing behind me.

Every Sunday morning since I was thirteen, I was expected to
mow my lawn and that of my elderly neighbors. I would wake up
hoping that my responsibility would magically disappear . . . only
to be disappointed by dad harping on me to get out of bed and start
mowing.

Starting with my backyard, I would rant to myself to blow off steam. I hate this. Why didn't I just say, "NO, I will not mow the lawn!"? This is so boring and repetitive. However, I eventually gave in to the therapeutic redundancy of the task, and the voice in my head soon quelled.

Push forward, pull back, pivot, again.

My Sunday morning thoughts always began with a resentment towards the task, later wandering to the discussions I had with my dad throughout that week. Our relationship was classic for that of two resolute individuals; we would get along swimmingly until one of us got a little too spirited during a politically charged debate or when one played devil's advocate a little too well. I would leave the discussion fuming, either frustrated that I couldn't articulate a point well enough or mad, knowing I was wrong but unwilling to admit it.

Next, I would mow my neighbor's lawn. Maybe I was over-reacting. This isn't even that bad. At least I'm breaking gender norms! Alone with my thoughts, focusing on the mundane task at hand, I soon learned that mowing the lawn was only as dull as I made it. I began to fill the empty time with reflections. Each time I pushed forward, I would reconsider my previous rhetoric. Each time I pulled back, I would think about why my dad said what he said. Each time I pivoted, I would reevaluate my initial conclusion. Each time I geared up to push forward again, I would pick out the lesson, enabling me to admit when I was defending the wrong.

Push forward, pull back, pivot, again.

The more I practiced reflecting, the easier it became for me to understand situations for what they were, rather than what the voice in my head insisted they were. Reflecting also gives me a chance to clear my head and build a nuanced approach to adversity. When I first pushed forward to pitch my anti-racism video newsletter, it was met with pushback from my school's administration. Apparently, it wasn't something our school needed. The BLM banner was good enough. Infuriated, I succumbed with an "I understand," even though the voice in my head disagreed. This is exactly what perpetuates systemic racism. Was I really in the wrong here? So, I pulled back to realize that the administrators had multiple stakeholders to account for and that I may have come off as too strong and inflexible. I pivoted to come up with a more comprehensive, win-win plan. When I geared up to push forward again, I presented a more integrative plan that was well received by my school's administrators, staff, and other students, thus beginning our collaboration in the Anti-Racism Working Group and video newsletter.

No longer do I need a lawn mower to reflect and get productive outcomes. All I have to remember is my simple mantra.

Push forward, pull back, pivot, again.

REVIEW

What did the essay do well?

Maia does a good job of sticking to a (not cliché) theme, "Push forward, pull back, pivot, again," which speaks to her convictions and ambition but also her foresight and maturity. Throughout the essay, using her lawn-mowing chore, debates with her father, and the Anti-Racism Working Group she launched, Maia lays out how she stayed true to herself without becoming inflexible and unreasonable. The passion for activism and social change that is the focus of Maia's essay is illustrated as she uses her chores and interaction with her father to craft a more complete narrative. The author ultimately strikes a balance in displaying both her dedication to her social causes and her ability to reflect upon her opinions. The incorporation of personal insights allows the reader to understand the aforementioned qualities that colleges are looking to include within their campus.

What could be improved about the essay?

There are moments in the prose where the language feels more stilted or rushed. One easy way to catch these snags in an essay's flow is to read it aloud as you edit: If anything feels unnatural to say, it should be edited to reflect more of your natural speaking voice so it shows more of your inherent character. The subjects of the essay also feel somewhat disjointed at times, and it may have made more sense to reorganize the essay so that Maia's working group was alluded to before the final section.

What made this essay memorable?

Maia does a great job balancing humor with gravity, using her refrain as a structural guide as well as a central theme. Her conclusion in particular leaves a lasting impact with its neat bookend. It's especially satisfying to read an essay that features one key accomplishment—a successful student-led initiative to launch an antiracism initiative—that never feels like a brag or too singular.

—Cara Chang

CONCLUSION

Successful essays are extremely diverse in topic, style, and sub-stance as evidenced by the variety in this book. Everyone has the capacity to write a great essay regardless of their life experiences, and there is no set formula for the perfect admissions essay. That being said, the essay is the most crucial element of your applica-tion, as it presents one of the limited chances to showcase to the admissions office who you truly are, going beyond the restrictions of your resume, transcript, and test scores. We hope you have been able to find inspiration from the essays and essay reviews in this book. While writing your own essay, keep in mind some key basics to make sure your essay is well written. Regardless of the topic you choose and the flair of your authorial voice, good essays generally are well organized, free of grammar and spelling errors, and have a clear focus or central theme. Make sure to proofread your essay or have other, trusted individuals review your essay to make sure that these elements of good writing are all achieved before you turn in your final product. Lastly, here are a few final pieces of advice from our contributors to help you craft your own successful college application essay.

I. CHOOSE A PERSONAL SUBJECT

While you may be overwhelmed after reviewing so many essays with different topics and struggling to figure out what exactly will set you apart to an Admissions Committee, it is important to remember that you already have all of the skills and experience necessary to write a great essay. The Admissions Committee is interested in learning about your personal qualities, values, and what communities or passions are most important to you. Beyond the other materials you will supply, take the time to showcase a part of your personality that might not be visible in your resume or course list. These qualities can be illustrated in a myriad of ways, as displayed by the diverse interests of the contributors to this book, so take the chance to be bold and write about something original even if it might not seem like the most conventional choice.

Don't try to impress the admission officers with a long list of accomplishments, be authentic and really try to show WHO you are through your essay. Are you ambitious or adventurous or caring? Whatever it might be, make sure it shines throughout your writing!

—**Marina S.**

Being vulnerable can also make the essay more compelling. You may choose to write about a deeply personal topic that you might otherwise not share with a stranger, but vulnerability will allow the reader to better connect with you. You should not feel pressured to hide your flaws or embellish stories about your experiences. Writing candidly is always a good idea, and you should not fear imperfection. It is great to demonstrate growth and acknowledge your flaws.

Be original. Do not fall into the trap of writing an essay to impress the admission officer. Everyone here at Harvard is so unique and so different from the rest. Show your true colors and do not be afraid.

—**Gred B.**

Never try to write as though you are someone else, as it will be clear to admissions officers and can only hurt your application. It can be tempting to glamorize and embellish your own accomplishments, but no one outside of the Admissions Committee can ever be 100 percent sure of the characteristics they are looking for and how they want to create their incoming class. Admissions Committees care about admitting applicants with integrity and those who are accepting and respectful, so do not do yourself a disservice by overstating or falsifying information.

Ultimately, it is your choice on what to showcase to Admissions Committees in the essay and an opportunity to explain why you would be a valuable addition to the student body. If you are still stuck, consider asking yourself how your experiences have shaped the person you are today and what stories you can use to illustrate that. You can think about what qualities or attributes you want readers to come away with after reading your essay and work backwards from there. For example, you might want to illustrate your creativity and compassion, or maybe you could highlight your resourcefulness and determination. Regardless of what you choose, having a clear and defined objective makes the process of brainstorming and drafting your essay easier.

II. GET CREATIVE: CRAFTING A UNIQUE STYLE

Essays can be elevated by dedicating careful attention to stylistic choices as you begin writing. Creative and unique styles can come in many forms. Many successful essays may use imagery, dialogue, or sensory details to strengthen their resonance with the reader. Sensory details can elevate a narrative by providing readers an image to pair with the events of the essay and are evidence of stronger writing skills, so as a general rule, the more details, the better. We grouped the essays in this book by general themes and topics, but without the strength of details, it can be difficult for readers to differentiate two applicants from one another. For example, if two students both write about overcoming the adversity of a sports injury, they should craft a strong narrative about their individual experiences rather than rely on vague, common ideas such as motivation and determination. Details can come into play in a variety of ways for the essay. For example, you can use descriptive details like Raymond does in the following excerpt to ground his storytelling that covers multiple days:

That day, and nearly every day for a week, I went to the hospital over three hours away to see her. During the long, sweltering drive one of those mornings, there was a period when I passed by miles of black-eyed Susans lining the median and sides of the highway. Although they were sparse at first—specks of beauty in an otherwise unassuming landscape—they soon grew to number in the thousands, obscuring the dried brown grass underneath with their golden petals.

—Raymond W.

Another way to incorporate details into the essay is by using dialogue. Think about the narrative techniques used in novels. Many writers take the idea of creating a narrative very seriously, and using short pieces of dialogue can bring a scene to life. For example, Orlee used bits of dialogue to engage the reader in her scene of bra shopping with her grandmother:

The saleswoman called to my grandmother from across the store, "What cup size is she?"

"I don't know," my grandmother screamed back. "Can you measure her?"

—Orlee M.

There are plenty of creative ways to tell your story through the essay. Having these details also assists the authentic aspect of your writing, which was covered in the first point.

III. KEEP YOUR MESSAGE IN MIND

As you craft your entire application in addition to the essay, it is a good tactic to have a clear message in mind of what you are hoping to relay to the Admissions Committee through your submitted materials. Whatever message you choose can range from qualities about you, such as grit and hard work, to your growth and learning style. It can be useful to think about your essay as one part of your entire application, and understanding the process of review that the Admissions Committee takes can help you strategize your approach to your essay. In most cases, there is one or a couple of readers who read your entire application and place the essay in context with the achievements outlined in your other materials. The essay is the place to make a lasting impression. In order to stand out from the many applications admissions officers read, your essay should speak directly to the reader and make your voice shine.

Within the admissions room, your application reader can advocate for you, saying that you are a strong, worthy applicant to the university. In turn, when writing your Common Application, show ample personality, to ensure that your admissions officer, who is a stranger, feels a strong connection to you and will advocate for your place at Harvard. For instance, I knew that my resume would speak to my political involvement, so I used my Common Application to highlight that I am goofy, musical, and family oriented.

—**Lauren P.**

An approach like Lauren's can be successful in maximizing the various opportunities and constrained space within your application to present yourself fully to the Admissions Committee.

Additionally, while it is important to have a clear sense of the message you hope to convey in your essay, you should make sure to avoid overemphasizing or repeating information that can be accessed in other parts of your application. It is a perfectly good choice to write about your involvement in a sport, club, or organization you are extremely passionate about, as some of the essays in this book have done. If an experience in such an organization or a class can provide a framework for you to write an essay that introduce aspects of yourself below the surface, go for it! However, as you can glean from many of the other essays showcased, essays can talk about more mundane experiences that are not focused on achievement. Regardless of the topic, writing with a clear intent can illuminate for essay readers what impression you hope to leave.

IV. WORDS OF ADVICE FROM OUR CONTRIBUTORS

We hope you have taken away some valuable insights from our book and feel more prepared to begin writing your own successful college application essay. Keep in mind that the college application process may be time-consuming and at times stressful, so we encourage you to find motivation and support from the pieces of advice our essay contributors have provided:

"An application reader walks towards their office with a stack of one hundred college essays without names on them. Your essay is one of them, and they trip and fall, causing all of the essays to scatter. Would your best friend be able to read your essay and know it is yours?" This piece of advice was the most essential I was given as an applicant. I was scared, stressed, nervous, and overwhelmed, not knowing what was special about me or what I had that made me "stick out," until I wasn't. All I knew is that I've done what I've done, and that is all I've got. And that's when I felt my application writing fall into place. All that time searching for that "perfect" topic was unnecessary as there is no such thing. The one thing I learned is authenticity always wins. I didn't write of a life-changing moment, or being the first to do anything, because I simply wasn't the first. Rather, I focused on my identity, what do I care about to my core? And since then, these essays, all compiled on one Google document, make me smile every time I see them, because I did right by myself. I know that I was chosen to go to whatever school based on their reading of who I am. It doesn't have to be a deep idea in others' eyes, but core to you—you just have to portray that and they'll see it. I smile because I know that this was the first time I can say that I have documented who I am in writing. And my best friend would find my essay in seconds.

—Reza S.

A college application is a very curated thing. In the process of crafting it, do not allow yourself to actually become reduced just to what is on those (digital) pages. Between academics, extracurriculars, work, and every other obligation in life that demands your time and attention, do not forget to stop and be HUMAN every once in a while. No matter how busy you think you are—you have the time for it, I promise! This can be difficult to internalize in the face of grind culture, which pressures you to devote every cell in your body to a "worthy" purpose, but in my humble opinion, the worthiest purpose of all something can have is to bring us joy. Take it from a fortune cookie I keep in my wallet: "Choosing what you want to do, and when to do it, is an act of creation."

—Raymond W.

Write about a cross section of your life for your personal essay. I would have had to compromise on many more parts of my identity writing about clinical research or public health than Barnes and Noble. Interests change, but the identity and passion that underlie them are bedrock.

—Abby Y.

Sometimes the most meaningful essays are about something small, where only you see the true meaning of it and how it connects to you and the rest of the world.

—Nour K.

Pursue activities you are truly passionate about in high school as opposed to doing something because it looks "good" on your resume.

—Alexander D.

Have confidence in yourself. Colleges are looking to admit applicants they believe will be engaged students, willing to learn and grow, and interesting individuals who can contribute to campus in a variety of social and extracurricular ways. Be honest and true to yourself throughout the process of writing because ultimately, you want to demonstrate who you truly are to your essay's readers. Good luck.

ACKNOWLEDGMENTS

The creation of this book was a collaborative effort, and I would like to extend my gratitude to the talented and dedicated individuals who made it possible. First and foremost, I would like to thank the publishing team at *The Harvard Crimson*—Libby Wu, Penelope Alegria, Daniel Berk, Summer Shen, Amy Huang, Matthew Sheridan, Sean Gallagher, Matthew Pantaleo, Ella Dotzler, and Claire Pak—for their incredible work in bringing this project to life. I would also like to express my gratitude to our Business Manager, Cynthia Lu, and our editor at St. Martin's Press, Christina Lopez, who provided invaluable support and guidance throughout the process. Finally, we would like to thank our contributors for generously sharing their personal stories with us, and our reviewers for offering additional insight into each essay.

Thank you all for your hard work, dedication, and support. We hope that this book will inspire and encourage future generations of college applicants to pursue their dreams with confidence and passion.

—Isabella Tran
Publishing Manager, 150th Guard of *The Harvard Crimson*

ABOUT *THE HARVARD CRIMSON*

The Harvard Crimson has been the daily newspaper of Harvard University since 1873. Published from Cambridge, Massachusetts, *The Crimson* is the nation's oldest continually operating daily college newspaper.